Policing the Internet

Other Books in the At Issue series:

Antidepressants
Are Conspiracy Theories Valid?
Are Privacy Rights Being Violated?
Child Labor and Sweatshops
Child Sexual Abuse
Creationism Versus Evolution
Does Advertising Promote Substance Abuse?
Does Outsourcing Harm America?
Does the World Hate the United States?
Do Nuclear Weapons Pose a Serious Threat?
Drug Testing
The Ethics of Capital Punishment
The Ethics of Genetic Engineering
The Ethics of Human Cloning
Gay and Lesbian Families
Gay Marriage
Gene Therapy
How Can Domestic Violence Be Prevented?
How Does Religion Influence Politics?
Hurricane Katrina
Is American Society Too Materialistic?
Is Poverty a Serious Threat?
Legalizing Drugs
Responding to the AIDS Epidemic
Steroids
What Causes Addiction?

At Issue

Policing the Internet

Peggy Daniels, Book Editor

GREENHAVEN PRESS
An imprint of Thomson Gale, a part of The Thomson Corporation

Detroit • New York • San Francisco • New Haven, Conn. • Waterville, Maine • London

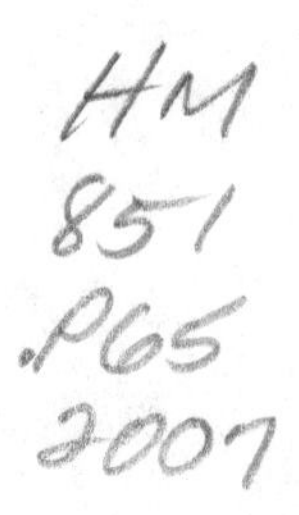

THOMSON
GALE

Christine Nasso, *Publisher*
Elizabeth Des Chenes, *Managing Editor*

For more information, contact:
Greenhaven Press
27500 Drake Rd.
Farmington Hills, MI 48331-3535
Or you can visit our Internet site at http://www.gale.com

Articles in Greenhaven Press anthologies are often edited for length to meet page requirements. In addition, original titles of these works are changed to clearly present the main thesis and to explicitly indicate the author's opinion. Every effort is made to ensure that Greenhaven Press accurately reflects the original intent of the authors. Every effort has been made to trace the owners of copyrighted material.

LIBRARY OF CONGRESS CATALOGING-IN-PUBLICATION DATA

Policing the Internet / Peggy Daniels, book editor.
p. cm. -- (At issue)
Includes bibliographical references and index.
ISBN-13: 978-0-7377-2733-3 (hardcover)
ISBN-13: 978-0-7377-2734-0 (pbk.)
1. Internet--Social aspects. 2. Computer crimes--Prevention. 3. Internet--Government policy. I. Daniels, Peggy.
HM851.P65 2007
354.75--dc22

2007004401

ISBN-10: 0-7377-2733-0 (hardcover)
ISBN-10: 0-7377-2734-9 (pbk.)

Printed in the United States of America
10 9 8 7 6 5 4 3 2 1

Contents

Introduction

For millions of people around the world, the Internet has become an indispensable part of everyday life. More than 100 million unique Web sites provide a seemingly endless array of news, entertainment, social networking, online shopping, and other services. E-mail and instant messages keep people connected to family, friends, and coworkers. Web-based university courses have broadened access to higher education, and online libraries allow students to work from the comfort of their rooms at home or in the dorm. The Internet has also transformed the employment landscape. The development of the Internet itself produces countless jobs, while corporations and governments are continually expanding the amount of business that is conducted online.

What was once seen as simply a novelty or a fun distraction is now viewed as a necessity of modern living. In April 2006 an estimated 73 percent of U.S. residents over the age of eighteen were Internet users, along with an estimated 87 percent of young people aged twelve to seventeen. The Internet has changed the way people communicate, learn, work, and relax. In a June 2006 Abritron/Edison survey, 62 percent of a sampling of U.S. Internet users stated that they would rather give up access to television than access to the Internet.

The Internet: Proceed with Caution

The dangers and perils of the Internet are frequently featured in news reports, and often used as the subject of movies and television crime dramas. The Internet world of identity theft, online predators, and e-mail con artists has developed its own language, with words like *spam* and *phishing* being newly added to the standard dictionary. Even the most casual Internet user is often aware of the Web's potential pitfalls.

Despite a growing awareness of the need for caution online, many young people are recklessly surfing the Web. In *Protecting Teens Online*, a 2005 survey of online teens and their parents, both groups agreed that teenagers do things online that they wouldn't want their parents to know about, and that teenagers aren't careful enough when sharing personal information online. The Internet's chat rooms and social-networking sites are excellent places for young people to connect with like-minded friends. But those same places also have the potential to expose teens to people who may not be what they seem.

"The Internet is a wonderful tool for communicating, gathering information and making transactions. However, it gives no privilege to good guys. The same technology that can help people find and resume relationships with long-lost friends can also bring predators into their lives. And the same tools that help those with rare forms of cancer build communities with fellow sufferers are also being used to support communities of pedophiles and to encourage teenage girls to become anorexic," Lee Rainie and John Horrigan commented in their 2005 analysis of Internet trends "Internet: The Mainstreaming of Online Life."

Online Security: A Critical Challenge

With all of its various services and sites, the Internet is a virtual community like any physical city or town. Most cities have dedicated law-enforcement agencies to patrol the streets and maintain order, but the Internet crosses international borders and presents unique challenges for the enforcement of international law. For example, the Internet company Yahoo! was entangled in a six-year lawsuit brought by the government of France, which sued Yahoo! for providing access to content that, although illegal by French law, is considered to be free speech that is protected in the United States by the First Amendment. "The case attracted immediate interest since it struck at the heart of one of the Internet's most challenging issues—how to bring the seemingly borderless Net to a world with borders," Michael Geist wrote in 2006 for *BBC News*.

Because people are spending more leisure and work time online than ever before, the security of the Internet has become a critical priority. Policing the Internet is a topic that holds worldwide interest as governments struggle to enforce local laws and social customs within the global Internet arena. In November 2006 the number of Internet users worldwide was estimated at more than 1 billion people. It would be difficult enough to police a city of that size, and policing a virtual community with that many members seems nearly impossible. Law-enforcement agencies and governments around the world continue to work together to find the best ways to police the Internet. But with the Internet's explosive growth and its increasing importance in global society, international law enforcement is just one step in the policing process.

Taking Responsibility

Effective Internet policing requires that individual users be made aware of potential online dangers and educated about things they can do to prevent themselves from being victimized. While legislation is important in the prosecution of crimes once they have been committed, crime prevention is equally important. "The biggest single weapon that governments can bring to bear is educating the public on how to use technology wisely," Brian White wrote in 2005 on Silicon.com. The real burden of policing the Internet may be in educating users to limit their vulnerability in the first place.

Savvy Internet users know that the same commonsense rules that work in the physical world also apply online. Don't reveal too much personal information to strangers. Don't give out passwords, account numbers, or other personal identifying information online. And if something seems too good to be true, it probably is not true. The Internet is an exciting, fun, and useful place, and with good sense and caution on the part of its users, it can stay that way.

1

The Internet Needs Policing

David Talbot

David Talbot is a chief correspondent for Technology Review. *He held a Knight Science Journalism Fellowship at the Massachusetts Institute of Technology (MIT) in 1999–2000 and has had a long career as a newspaper reporter. Talbot has received numerous awards for journalism, including honors from the Overseas Press Club of America and the International Press Association.*

There are basic problems in the fundamental design of the Internet. Originally intended as a simple communications network, the Internet has grown to include complicated new technology. The addition of this technology has resulted in more opportunities for malicious attacks. Security holes have been filled with software patches, but there are now so many different patches that it is almost impossible to keep track of them all. The focus on keeping the Internet safe for everyone has taken time away from the creation of innovative new features and applications. A better, safer, more secure global network is needed.

The Internet has wrought wonders: e-commerce has flourished, and e-mail has become a ubiquitous means of communication. Almost one billion people now use the Internet, and critical industries like banking increasingly rely on it. At the same time, the Internet's shortcomings have resulted in plunging security and a decreased ability to accommodate new technologies. "We are at an inflection point, a revolution

David Talbot, "The Internet Is Broken," *Technology Review*, December–January 2005–2006, pp. 63–65, 67–69.

point," [Internet elder statesman and onetime chief protocol architect David] Clark . . . argues. And he delivers a strikingly pessimistic assessment of where the Internet will end up without dramatic intervention. "We might just be at the point where the utility of the Internet stalls—and perhaps turns downward."

Indeed, for the average user, the Internet these days all too often resembles New York's Times Square in the 1980s. It was exciting and vibrant, but you made sure to keep your head down, lest you be offered drugs, robbed, or harangued by the insane. Times Square has been cleaned up, but the Internet keeps getting worse, both at the user's level, and—in the view of Clark and others—deep within its architecture. Over the years, as Internet applications proliferated—wireless devices, peer-to-peer file-sharing, telephony—companies and network engineers came up with ingenious and expedient patches, plugs, and workarounds. The result is that the originally simple communications technology has become a complex and convoluted affair. For all of the Internet's wonders, it is also difficult to manage and more fragile with each passing day.

A New Internet?

That's why Clark argues that it's time to rethink the Internet's basic architecture, to potentially start over with a fresh design—and equally important, with a plausible strategy for proving the design's viability, so that it stands a chance of implementation. "It's not as if there is some killer technology at the protocol or network level that we somehow failed to include," says Clark. "We need to take all the technologies we already know and fit them together so that we get a different overall system. This is not about building a technology innovation that changes the world but about architecture—pulling the pieces together in a different way to achieve high-level objectives."

Just such an approach is now gaining momentum, spurred on by the National Science Foundation [NSF]. NSF managers are working to forge a five-to-seven-year plan estimated to cost $200 million to $300 million in research funding to develop clean-slate architectures that provide security, accommodate new technologies, and are easier to manage. They also hope to develop an infrastructure that can be used to prove that the new system is really better than the current one. "If we succeed in what we are trying to do, this is bigger than anything we, as a research community, have done in computer science so far," says Guru Parulkar, an NSF program manager involved with the effort. "In terms of its mission and vision, it is a very big deal. But now we are just at the beginning. It has the potential to change the game. It could take it to the next level in realizing what the Internet could be that has not been possible because of the challenges and problems." . . .

Security Problems

These days, improving the utility of the Internet is not so much about delivering the latest cool application; it's about survival. In August [2005], IBM released a study reporting that "virus-laden e-mails and criminal-driven security attacks" leapt by 50 percent in the first half of 2005, with government and the financial-services, manufacturing, and healthcare industries in the crosshairs. In July [2005], the Pew Internet and American Life Project reported that 43 percent of U.S. Internet users—59 million adults—reported having spyware or adware on their computers, thanks merely to visiting websites. (In many cases, they learned this from the sudden proliferation of error messages or freeze-ups.) Fully 91 percent had adopted some defensive behavior—avoiding certain kinds of websites, say, or not downloading software. "Go to a neighborhood bar, and people are talking about firewalls. That was just not true three years ago," says Susannah Fox, associate director of the Pew project.

Then there is spam. One leading online security company, Symantec, says that between July 1 and December 31, 2004, spam surged 77 percent at companies that Symantec monitored. The raw numbers are staggering: weekly spam totals on average rose from 800 million to more than 1.2 billion messages, and 60 percent of all e-mail was spam, according to Symantec. But perhaps most menacing of all are "botnets"—collections of computers hijacked by hackers to do remote-control tasks like sending spam or attacking websites. This kind of wholesale hijacking—made more potent by wide adoption of always-on broadband connections—has spawned hardcore crime: digital extortion. Hackers are threatening destructive attacks against companies that don't meet their financial demands. According to a study by a Carnegie Mellon University researcher, 17 of 100 companies surveyed had been threatened with such attacks.

A well-placed attack could trigger a costly blackout that would cripple part of the country.

Increasing Threats

Simply put, the Internet has no inherent security architecture—nothing to stop viruses or spam or anything else. Protections like firewalls and antispam software are add-ons, security patches in a digital arms race. The President's Information Technology Advisory Committee, a group stocked with a who's who of infotech CEOs and academic researchers, says the situation is bad and getting worse. "Today, the threat clearly is growing," the council wrote in a report issued in early 2005. "Most indicators and studies of the frequency, impact, scope, and cost of cyber security incidents—among both organizations and individuals—point to continuously increasing levels and varieties of attacks." And we haven't even seen a real act of cyberterror, the "digital Pearl Harbor" memorably predicted by former White House counterterrorism czar Richard Clarke in 2000. Consider the nation's electrical grid: it relies on continuous network-based communications between power plants and grid managers to maintain a balance between production and demand. A well-placed attack could trigger a costly blackout that would cripple part of the country. The conclusion of the advisory council's report could not have been starker: "The IT [information technology] infrastructure is highly vulnerable to premeditated attacks with potentially catastrophic effects."

The system functions as well as it does only because of "the forbearance of the virus authors themselves," says Jonathan Zittrain, who cofounded the Berkman Center for Internet and Society at Harvard Law School and holds the Chair in Internet Governance and Regulation at the University of Oxford. "With one or two additional lines of code . . . the viruses could wipe their hosts' hard drives clean or quietly insinuate false data into spreadsheets or documents. Take any of the top ten viruses and add a bit of poison to them, and most of the world wakes up on a Tuesday morning unable to surf the Net—or finding much less there if it can."

Problems with Patches

The Internet's original protocols, forged in the late 1960s, were designed to do one thing very well: facilitate communication between a few hundred academic and government users. The protocols efficiently break digital data into simple units called packets and send the packets to their destinations through a series of network routers. Both the routers and PCs, also called nodes, have unique digital addresses known as Internet Protocol or IP addresses. That's basically it. The system assumed that all users on the network could be trusted and that the computers linked by the Internet were mostly fixed objects.

The Internet's design was indifferent to whether the information packets added up to a malicious virus or a love letter; it had no provisions for doing much besides getting the data to its destination. Nor did it accommodate nodes that moved—such as PDAs [personal digital assistants] that could connect to the Internet at any of myriad locations. Over the years, a slew of patches arose: firewalls, antivirus software, spam filters, and the like. One patch assigns each mobile node a new IP [Internet protocol] address every time it moves to a new point in the network.

Clearly, security patches aren't keeping pace. That's partly because different people use different patches and not everyone updates them religiously; some people don't have any installed. And the most common mobility patch—the IP addresses that constantly change as you move around—has downsides. When your mobile computer has a new identity every time it connects to the Internet, the websites you deal with regularly won't know it's you. This means, for example, that your favorite airline's Web page might not cough up a reservation form with your name and frequent-flyer number already filled out. The constantly changing address also means you can expect breaks in service if you are using the Internet to, say, listen to a streaming radio broadcast on your PDA. It also means that someone who commits a crime online using a mobile device will be harder to track down.

In the view of many experts in the field, there are even more fundamental reasons to be concerned. Patches create an ever more complicated system, one that becomes harder to manage, understand, and improve upon. "We've been on a track for 50 years of incrementally making improvements to the Internet and fixing problems that we see," says Larry Peterson, a computer scientist at Princeton University. "We see vulnerability, we try to patch it. That approach is one that has worked for 50 years. But there is reason to be concerned. Without a long-term plan, if you are just patching the next problem you see, you end up with an increasingly complex and brittle system. It makes new services difficult to employ. It makes it much harder to manage because of the added complexity of all these point solutions that have been added. At the same time, there is concern that we will hit a dead end at some point. There will be problems we can't sufficiently patch."

Patches create an ever more complicated system, one that becomes harder to manage, understand, and improve upon.

Change Is Needed

The patchwork approach draws complaints even from the founder of a business that is essentially an elaborate and ingenious patch for some of the Internet's shortcomings. Tom Leighton is cofounder and chief scientist of Akamai, a company that ensures that its clients' Web pages and applications are always available, even if huge numbers of customers try to log on to them or a key fiber-optic cable is severed. Akamai closely monitors network problems, strategically stores copies of a client's website at servers around the world, and accesses those servers as needed. But while his company makes its money from patching the Net, Leighton says the whole system needs fundamental architectural change. "We are in the mode of trying to plug holes in the dike," says Leighton, an MIT [Massachusetts Institute of Technology] mathematician who is also a member of the President's Information Technology Advisory Committee and chair of its Cyber Security Subcommittee. "There are more and more holes, and more resources are going to plugging the holes, and there are less resources being devoted to fundamentally changing the game, to changing the Internet."

When Leighton says "resources," he's talking about billions of dollars. Take Microsoft, for example. Its software mediates between the Internet and the PC. These days, of the $6 billion that Microsoft spends annually on research and development, approximately one-third, or $2 billion, is directly spent on security efforts. "The evolution of the Internet, the development of threats from the Internet that could attempt to intrude on systems—whether Web servers, Web browsers, or e-mail-based threats—really changed the equation," says Steve Lipner, Microsoft's director of security strategy and engineering strategy. "Ten years ago, I think people here in the industry were designing software for new features, new performance, ease of use, what have you. Today, we train everybody for security." Not only does this focus on security siphon resources from other research, but it can even hamper research that does get funded. Some innovations have been kept in the lab, Lipner says, because Microsoft couldn't be sure they met security standards.

Things will slowly get worse and might get so bad that people won't use the Internet as much as they might like.

Of course, some would argue that Microsoft is now scrambling to make up for years of selling insecure products. But the Microsoft example has parallels elsewhere. Eric Brewer, director of Intel's Berkeley, CA, research lab, notes that expenditures on security are like a "tax" and are "costing the nation billions and billions of dollars." This tax shows up as increased product prices, as companies' expenditures on security services and damage repair, as the portion of processor speed and storage devoted to running defensive programs, as the network capacity consumed by spam, and as the costs to the average person trying to dodge the online minefield of buying the latest firewalls. "We absolutely can leave things alone. But it has this continuous 30 percent tax, and the tax might go up," Brewer says. "The penalty for not [fixing] it isn't immediately fatal. But things will slowly get worse and might get so bad that people won't use the Internet as much as they might like."

A New Architecture

The existing Internet architecture also stands in the way of new technologies. Networks of intelligent sensors that collectively monitor and interpret things like factory conditions, the weather, or video images could change computing as much as cheap PCs did 20 years ago. But they have entirely different communication requirements. "Future networks aren't going to be PCs docking to mainframes. It's going to be about some car contacting the car next to it. All of this is happening in an embedded context. Everything is machine to machine rather than people to people," says Dipankar Raychaudhuri, director of the Wireless Information Network Laboratory (Winlab) at Rutgers University. With today's architecture, making such a vision reality would require more and more patches.

It would be a huge boon to Internet security if you could be sure an e-mail from your bank is really from your bank and not a scam artist, and if the bank could be sure that when someone logs in to your account, that person is really you and not someone who stole your account number.

When Clark talks about creating a new architecture, he says the job must start with the setting of goals. First, give the medium a basic security architecture—the ability to authenticate whom you are communicating with and prevent things like spam and viruses from ever reaching your PC. Better security is "the most important motivation for this redesign," Clark says. Second, make the new architecture practical by devising protocols that allow Internet service providers to better route traffic and collaborate to offer advanced services without compromising their businesses. Third, allow future computing devices of any size to connect to the Internet—not just PCs but sensors and embedded processors. Fourth, add technology that makes the network easier to manage and more resilient. For example, a new design should allow all pieces of the network to detect and report emerging problems—whether technical breakdowns, traffic jams, or replicating worms—to network administrators.

Improved Security

The good news is that some of these goals are not so far off. NSF has, over the past few years, spent more than $30 million supporting and planning such research. Academic and corporate research labs have generated a number of promising technologies: ways to authenticate who's online; ways to identify criminals while protecting the privacy of others; ways to add wireless devices and sensors. While nobody is saying that any single one of these technologies will be included in a new architecture, they provide a starting point for understanding what a "new" Internet might actually look like and how it would differ from the old one.

Some promising technologies that might figure into this new architecture are coming from PlanetLab, which Princeton's Peterson has been nurturing in recent years. In this still-growing project, researchers throughout the world have been developing software that can be grafted onto today's dumb Internet routers. One example is software that "sniffs" passing Internet traffic for worms. The software looks for telltale packets sent out by worm-infected machines searching for new hosts and can warn system administrators of infections. Other software prototypes detect the emergence of data traffic jams and come up with more efficient ways to reroute traffic around them. These kinds of algorithms could become part of a fundamental new infrastructure, Peterson says.

A second set of technologies could help authenticate Internet communications. It would be a huge boon to Internet security if you could be sure an e-mail from your bank is really from your bank and not a scam artist, and if the bank could be sure that when someone logs in to your account, that person is really you and not someone who stole your account number.

Today, the onus of authentication is on the Internet user, who is constantly asked to present information of various kinds: passwords, social-security numbers, employee ID numbers, credit card numbers, frequent-flyer numbers, PIN numbers, and so on. But when millions of users are constantly entering these gate-opening numbers, it makes it that much easier for spyware, or a thief sniffing wireless Internet traffic, to steal, commit fraud, and do damage.

One evolving solution, developed by Internet2—a research consortium based in Ann Arbor, MI, that develops advanced Internet technologies for use by research laboratories and universities—effectively creates a middleman who does the job. Called Shibboleth, the software mediates between a sender and a recipient; it transmits the appropriate ID numbers, passwords, and other identifying information to the right recipients for you, securely, through the centralized exchange of digital certificates and other means. In addition to making the dispersal of information more secure, it helps protect privacy. That's because it discloses only the "attributes" of a person pertinent to a particular transaction, rather than the person's full "identity."

Right now, Shibboleth is used by universities to mediate access to online libraries and other resources; when you log on, the university knows your "attribute"—you are an enrolled student—and not your name or other personal information. This basic concept can be expanded: your employment status could open the gates to your company's servers; your birth date could allow you to buy wine online. A similar scheme could give a bank confidence that online account access is legitimate and conversely give a bank customer confidence that banking communications are really from the bank.

Shibboleth and similar technologies in development can, and do, work as patches. But some of their basic elements could also be built into a replacement Internet architecture. "Most people look at the Internet as such a dominant force, they only think how they can make it a little better," Clark says. "I'm saying, 'Hey, think about the future differently. What should our communications environment of 10 to 15 years from now look like? What is your goal?'"

A Challenging Task

It's worth remembering that despite all of its flaws, all of its architectural kluginess and insecurity and the costs associated with patching it, the Internet still gets the job done. Any effort to implement a better version faces enormous practical problems: all Internet service providers would have to agree to change all their routers and software, and someone would have to foot the bill, which will likely come to many billions of dollars. But NSF isn't proposing to abandon the old network or to forcibly impose something new on the world. Rather, it essentially wants to build a better mousetrap, show that it's better, and allow a changeover to take place in response to user demand. . . .

Still, skeptics claim that a smarter network could be even more complicated and thus failure-prone than the original bare-bones Internet. . . . "I'm not happy with the current state of affairs. I'm not happy with spam; I'm not happy with the amount of vulnerability to various forms of attack," says Vinton Cerf, one of the inventors of the Internet's basic protocols, who recently joined Google with a job title created just for him: chief Internet evangelist. "I do want to distinguish that the primary vectors causing a lot of trouble are penetrating holes in operating systems. It's more like the operating systems don't protect themselves very well. An argument could be made, 'Why does the network have to do that?'"

According to Cerf, the more you ask the network to examine data—to authenticate a person's identity, say, or search for viruses—the less efficiently it will move the data around. "It's really hard to have a network-level thing do this stuff, which means you have to assemble the packets into something bigger and thus violate all the protocols," Cerf says. "That takes a heck of a lot of resources." Still, Cerf sees value in the new NSF initiative. "If Dave Clark . . . sees some notions and ideas that would be dramatically better than what we have, I think that's important and healthy," Cerf says. "I sort of wonder about something, though. The collapse of the Net, or a major security disaster, has been predicted for a decade now." And of course no such disaster has occurred. . . .

The NSF effort to make the medium smarter also runs up against the libertarian culture of the Internet, says Harvard's Zittrain. "The NSF program is a worthy one in the first instance because it begins with the premise that the current Net has outgrown some of its initial foundations and associated tenets," Zittrain says. "But there is a risk, too, that any attempt to rewrite the Net's technical constitution will be so much more fraught, so much more self-conscious of the nontechnical matters at stake, that the cure could be worse than the problem."

The Internet's perennial problems are getting worse, at the same time that society's dependence on it is deepening.

Still, Zittrain sees hazards ahead if some sensible action isn't taken. He posits that the Internet's security problems, and the theft of intellectual property, could produce a counterreaction that would amount to a clampdown on the medium—everything from the tightening of software makers' control over their operating systems to security lockdowns by businesses. And of course, if a "digital Pearl Harbor" does occur, the federal government is liable to respond reflexively with heavy-handed reforms and controls. If such tightenings happen, Zittrain believes we're bound to get an Internet that is, in his words, "more secure—and less interesting."

Seeing a Different Future

But what all sides agree on is that the Internet's perennial problems are getting worse, at the same time that society's dependence on it is deepening. Just a few years ago, the work of researchers like Peterson didn't garner wide interest outside the networking community. But these days, Clark and Peterson are giving briefings to Washington policymakers. "There is recognition that some of these problems are potentially quite serious. You could argue that they have always been there," Peterson says. "But there is a wider recognition in the highest level of the government that this is true. We are getting to the point where we are briefing people in the president's Office of Science and Technology Policy. I specifically did, and other people are doing that as well. As far as I know, that's pretty new."

Outside the door to Clark's office at MIT, a nametag placed by a prankster colleague announces it to be the office of Albus Dumbledore—the wise headmaster of the Hogwarts School of Witchcraft and Wizardry, a central figure in the Harry Potter books. But while Clark in earlier years may have wrought some magic, helping transform the original Internet protocols into a robust communications technology that changed the world, he no longer has much control over what happens next.

But "because we don't have power, there is a greater chance that we will be left alone to try," he says. And so Clark, like Dumbledore, clucks over new generations of technical wizards. "My goal in calling for a fresh design is to free our minds from the current constraints, so we can envision a different future," he says. "The reason I stress this is that the Internet is so big, and so successful, that it seems like a fool's errand to send someone off to invent a different one." Whether the end result is a whole new architecture—or just an effective set of changes to the existing one—may not matter in the end. Given how entrenched the Internet is, the effort will have succeeded, he says, if it at least gets the research community working toward common goals, and helps "impose [and] creep in the right direction."

2

Teenagers Need Policing Online

Vicki Haddock

Vicki Haddock is a journalist and staff writer for the San Francisco Chronicle.

Using the Internet is one of the most popular recreational activities for teenagers. Many Internet sites are fun and safe for teens, but there are also many dangerous sides of the Internet. Significant problems have occurred for teens online, including cyberbullying, illegal gambling, substance abuse, self-destructive behavior, computer game addiction, and inappropriate use of social networking sites. Parents should be aware of their teens' online activity in order to teach teens about responsible, appropriate use of the Internet.

The Internet once was seen as a golden "information superhighway" transporting the next generation to the Promised Land. Now it may feel more like a minefield—seductive on the surface, but seeded with subterranean hazards.

Few families have escaped the warning sirens about sexual predators stalking children via the computer. It's hard to miss those . . . billboards claiming that 1 in 5 children has been sexually solicited online, although only a tiny fraction of those involve aggressive solicitations from someone believed to be over age 25. What experts fear is that parents remain relatively unaware of the much more ordinary hazards for their children in cyberspace:

- Online bullying, with kids taking harassment from the playground to an exponentially wider audience.
- Profiteers who run online pharmacy and gambling sites—and couldn't care less about the ages of their customers.
- Computer addiction, as players of elaborate online games such as World of Warcraft and City of Heroes become hopelessly obsessed.
- Web sites in which teens reinforce self-destructive behavior—for example, "Friends of Ana" sites advocating anorexia.
- Blog blowback from hip cyber social registers such as the wildly popular MySpace.com, in which kids become confessors and poseurs—at their peril.

American parents always have fretted over the newest recreation fad. A quarter century ago, they worried that Pac-Man and Donkey Kong fostered attention deficit disorder. A century ago, they panicked that a new pool table would trigger truancy, tobacco use and trouble in River City.

Defenders of cyberspace—including its frequent young inhabitants—say it encourages creativity and personal expression, and helps kids with similar interests connect across the globe, in a forum where race, accent and other physical attributes are irrelevant.

Fair enough. But adults and kids alike should be aware of potential pitfalls.

Cyberbullying

San Francisco, California's Washington High is still recovering from an incident in November [2005] in which a cyberbully hacked into the school's Web site to humiliate a single student. For several hours, while administrators scrambled to block it, the school site featured an obscene photo montage of the student's face superimposed on other bodies—labeled with his name, a racial slur and gang slogans.

"It was awful—enough to make you feel physically ill just looking at it," said Principal Andrew Ishibashi. "And of course word of it spread all around the school."

Investigators have yet to pinpoint the perpetrator.

"When I do school presentations, this always comes up as the number 1 problem," said attorney Parry Aftab, executive director of the nonprofit WiredSafety.org. "Lots of kids think it's worse to be bullied online than in person. If you know somebody intends to sock you in the face in the schoolyard, you might be able to avoid them, take a different hallway, follow a different route home. But cyberbullying follows you wherever you go—to your new school, to your grandmother's house."

Whereas brawn is a prerequisite for schoolyard bullies, cyberbullies can come in all shapes and sizes.

Adolescents—particularly girls—have long exploited the rumor mill to humiliate a social outcast or a rival for a boy's attention. The Web ups the ante.

While almost half of kids had been bullied online, 58 percent never told an adult about it.

There are the online polls inviting participants to post salacious or critical assessments of their classmates—as in "Who's the sluttiest girl at school?" or "Reasons to Hate Alex." There are the double agents who entice teens into e-mail chats about their crushes, fears, embarrassments—and then post them for public ridicule. There are the sneaks who use camera phones to take other students' pictures naked in the locker room and then display them online.

The parents of Vermont 13-year-old Ryan Halligan had warned him not to talk to strangers online. In retrospect, his own classmates posed a graver threat. Silently he endured months of their online torture—pronouncements like "You're a loser!" Eventually, he began threatening to take his own life.

"Tonight's the night," he typed.

"It's about time," came the response.

Ryan had the last word: he hanged himself.

One victim who became a crusader is Samantha Hahn, the National American Miss for 2005. Her saga began in sixth grade, when her best friend started a rumor that Samantha was a lesbian. Soon a circle of girls who dubbed themselves "the Evil Angels" were working around the clock to make Samatha's life hell.

The label followed her to three schools.

"Even now there are nights I relive the negative experiences in my dreams," she shared online. "They can hide behind a screen name, remaining anonymous while the victim becomes increasingly vulnerable and defenseless. . . . I received instant messages and e-mails saying, 'We're going to kill you'; 'I wouldn't go to the bathroom alone if I were you'; and 'you better watch your back.'"

A survey by the nonprofit i-SAFE America found that while almost half of kids had been bullied online, 58 percent never told an adult about it.

Drugs and Gambling

When 17-year-old Ryan Haight of La Mesa, California (San Diego County), used the computer in his family's den to order painkillers online, court reports indicate that 100 tablets of hydrocodone (a generic version of Vicodin) arrived in the mail a few days later, c.o.d.—despite the fact that he had no valid prescription.

And when his mother discovered him lifeless in his own bed from an overdose of a variety of drugs, including morphine, which he purchased online, it was another chilling reminder that not all online predators are seeking sex.

Instead these predators are in the pursuit of profit, and they often strike a bonanza among younger computer users who know how to access their parents' credit card or PayPal accounts, but not how to spot a scam.

The Haight case helped prompt several Internet search engines to ban advertising from unlicensed pharmacies. Nonetheless, the federal Drug Enforcement Administration continues to dismantle rogue pharmacies, including one operation that agents say was illegally distributing more than 3.5 million doses of heavily controlled substances per month.

A bill sponsored by Sen. Dianne Feinstein, D-Calif., would demand disclosure of the pharmacists connected to such sites and prohibit them from referring customers to doctors who write prescriptions based on online questionnaires without ever seeing their patients.

Age also poses little barrier to teens who—although they would be shown the door in Vegas—can slip into an online casino.

The proliferation of virtually unregulated cyber gambling has led to an increase in the number of problem gamblers between the ages of 11 and 19 seeking counseling. About a quarter of them start playing online games of chance for free, get hooked, then graduate up to actual wagering. Teen gamblers—lacking impulse control—are three times more likely to become addicted than adults, according to a Harvard Medical School study.

Computer Addiction

Trask Dunlap says he's quite confident he's not addicted to computer games.

Yes, the Petaluma, California, 18-year-old averages six hours per day playing the intricate online fantasy game World of Warcraft. Yes, for him a social gathering may involve some friends who are fellow gamers hauling their computers to his house for an all-night marathon. Yes, he recently logged 37 consecutive hours of play—stopping only for bathroom breaks, gulps of a Rockstar energy drink and a quick run to Jack in the Box.

But, he insisted, "I know myself, and I know I could quit anytime."

Therapists report a growing clientele with symptoms of obsessive-compulsive behavior linked to the computer.

His parents, psychotherapists Peter and Margaret Dunlap, aren't so sure. They see their son as an otherwise great kid who is developing an unhealthy screen obsession.

"To me it is addiction—a human cul-de-sac that doesn't lead to freedom and joy or meaning," said his father, who worries that Trask has trouble "finding the outdoors."

The family lives in the country and hasn't had TV reception for years. His parents now regret allowing Trask to start playing GameBoy at age 5. He counters that their restrictive strategy backfired and merely enhanced the computer's appeal—likening it to a little kid who is forbidden to pour his own pancake syrup and thus never learns for himself how much is too much. A few months ago, chafing at their restrictions on his computer time, he tested out of high school and moved in with a fellow computer gamer.

There is debate in the social sciences about whether people actually suffer computer "addiction"—a word that constitutes a strict diagnosis in the psychiatric world—although therapists report a growing clientele with symptoms of obsessive compulsive behavior linked to the computer. Maressa Orzack, a clinical psychologist who runs the Computer Addiction Study Center at Harvard's McLean Hospital, now estimates more than 1 in 10 gamers develop addiction—and says the most susceptible tend to be "really bright kids. . . . who are feeling overwhelmed by other factors in their lives."

On her list of symptoms indicating unhealthy dependence on the computer: feeling irritable or depressed when away from it; spending increased time and money on computer activities; and neglecting work, school or family obligations.

Among those who have researched online games, Nick Yee provides a positive assessment. While pursuing a doctorate in the communications department at Stanford University, he also runs his own Web site where he has collected years of his own studies and essays about computers—indicating, for example, that many gamers report gaining real-life skills—leadership, crisis management, logistical planning—from role-playing when, for example, they've commandeered a medieval army to slay cyberdragons.

"It's a great equalizer because it's totally merit-based," he said. "Where in the world outside of games can a 15-year-old lead a team of adults?"

Or, as Trask would say, users find computer games "definitely not mind-numbing—quite the opposite." Recently, economic circumstances led him to move back home and he's taking classes at Santa Rosa Junior College, although his World of Warcraft devotion still leads to household battles.

"My concern," said his mother, "is that the computer is taking him away from his life."

Self-Destructive Behavior

"Don't enter here unless you want to be a cut above!" declares one Web site offering hundreds of posts from mostly young members trying to be just that. Participants are into self-injury and mutilation—some trying to stop, but many others encouraging the practice.

"Yes, yes, feel the agony to the max—let the pain take you so low that you've never been so high," writes one girl who identifies herself as 16 and describes the exquisite psychic rewards she gets from the feel of a blade on her skin.

The beauty and danger of online communities is that teenagers can use searches and tags to connect with peers who share their interests—be it Bible study or environmental activism or self-destructive neuroses. Hundreds of cyberforums orbit around anorexia, bulimia, drug addiction and the like, created by and for kids with similar preoccupations.

It is helpful for many of those teens to know they're not alone. . . . However, these sites also give them a disordered, skewed slant on what normative behavior is like.

Some of these espouse the philosophy that kids can overcome such disorders in part by revealing their private struggles with those who are similarly struggling. But such sites are outnumbered by others in which participants call their choices "lifestyle options," not mental disorders—and display hostility toward parents, doctors and counselors trying to help them recover.

A typical pro-Ana [the belief that anorexia nervosa is not a disease but a lifestyle choice] site embracing anorexia, for example, displays photos of bony celebrities and hundreds of "thinspiration" quotations:

"All the food you eat will rot in your stomach, let it rot on the plate instead."

"Quod mi nutruit, mi destruit"—Latin for what nourishes me, destroys me.

"A flat stomach won't suffice—only a Concave one means Perfection."

"I want to walk in the snow and leave no footprints."

Stanford researchers are pioneering ways to assess such sites, with early results indicating that visitors don't necessarily have a sicker profile than other anorexics, even though they do glean new techniques to perpetuate eating disorders.

"It is helpful for many of these teens to know they're not alone. . . . However, these sites also give them a disordered, skewed slant on what normative behavior is like," said Rebecka Peebles, instructor in adolescent medicine at Lucile Packard Children's Hospital. She is the co-author of the first study of the phenomenon, with medical student Jenny Wilson. "My sense is these Web sites are not a vector for contagion . . . but I worry that they can, in vulnerable people, reinforce very unhealthy ideas."

Social Networking

Teens and even pre-teens know Web sites like MySpace, Xanga, Bebo and Facebook as network neighborhoods to intersect with peers and design their own profile pages—indeed, their own "images"—from the ground up. But browse these sites and it becomes clear that many of the participants are operating on the fallacious assumption that only their like-minded friends will ever see their sites.

Such was the case with the 12-year-old daughter of Stefan Wever of San Francisco, California.

On a whim last November, Wever decided to view the page his daughter had crafted for herself on MySpace. What popped up horrified him: a photo of her dressed up in a provocative pose, alongside explicit lyrics, and the declaration that she was 18 years old. The piece de resistance was her [display name]: "La Loca Prostituta."

Confronted by her parents, the girl tearfully contended that everyone in her class made similar postings, and that she lied about her age to be allowed access to MySpace (users must enter a birth date indicating they are at least 14, although this is not verified).

Wever surmised that his daughter wasn't serious—but he knew just how easily her post could be misinterpreted. "I logged onto her MySpace, replaced her photo with a very scary looking picture of me, changed the caption to

GROUNDED and wrote in her profile that I was her father and was very disappointed in my daughter, that she had betrayed the trust we had in her, and was placing herself in potentially grave danger."

The parents also restricted their daughter's computer access—homework only—for half a year, forbidding her from using a computer at any friend's house.

The environment encourages kids to be far more suggestive online than they would feel comfortable being in real life.

And their relationship since is better, Wever insisted. "She knew we generally trusted her judgment, but this one time she had really let us down."

MySpace may appear to be a free, cozy network run by an amiable guy named Tom, but actually it's fast approaching 50 million members and is owned by right-wing media mogul Rupert Murdoch, who paid a cool $580 million to add it to his portfolio of conservative tabloids and Fox News. He was clever enough to retain co-founders Tom Anderson and Chris De Wolfe to give the patina of edginess.

Users don't just lie about their ages—many desperately try to look and sound older as well, which in their immature worldview often means liberally using the f-word, striking lots of "come hither" lingerie poses and boasting about precisely how wasted they got over the weekend. Clearly a large proportion of posts are partially fake—there can't be that many teenagers aspiring to become serial killers or strippers.

"I think adults would overreact [if] they started randomly browsing profiles because . . . it's just kids messing around," said Xanga aficionado Justin Skyles, a San Jose, California ninth-grader. "I think kids could probably spot what's true and what's not, but parents don't really have any business in that zone because they might just freak out over nothing."

Concerned adults say such sites feed into a culture that prizes vulgarity over meaningful communication and treats girls, in particular, as sex objects. The environment encourages kids to be far more suggestive online than they would feel comfortable being in real life. And of course such sites offer a virtual shopping mall of victims to predators, who can browse for someone just in their taste, age range and neighborhood, and glean tips on how to lure them in. ("You a fan of Kurt Cobain? Nirvana so rocked!")

Few young users of such sites realize that parents increasingly peruse these pages, private school administrators have expelled students for postings, and police officers have picked up information to bust keggers and drug deals.

And personal pages—even old, deleted postings that nonetheless are archived and therefore accessible—could become part of a background check when teenagers apply for colleges, scholarships and jobs. Some firms hired to run background checks on applicants already are data-mining such sites.

Parents Should Supervise Teens Online

The 21st century seems locked in a struggle to balance freedom and privacy against safety and security. Nationally, that debate revolves around terrorism. At home, it's all about the computer.

Families are straining to negotiate their own compromises. How much parental supervision is required? How much time online is too much? Should kids surrender their passwords?

Parents at least need to keep in mind a checklist of danger signs, including kids who spend increasing amounts of time online, who seem furtive about their online pursuits or whose attitude changes radically. Internet filtering software helps, but it isn't foolproof—and can be thwarted by computer-savvy users.

More and more parents are checking in on sites like MySpace, which provide a window into the world of their sons and daughters.

Still others—call them diligent or suspicious—are resorting to sophisticated software that can reconstruct every keystroke. Programs such as PC Tattletale, which can be downloaded for a free trial, captures screen shots every four seconds.

Cyberspace can be an eye-opening, fun and even magical place to explore. But young voyagers—and wise parents of those sojourners—must be keenly aware of the terrain, and even more careful of where they step.

3

Government Should Regulate the Internet

Ronald J. Mann and Seth R. Belzley

Ronald J. Mann is an expert in commercial law and e-commerce. He is the founder and codirector of the Center for Law, Business, and Economics, and is also a member of the American Law Institute. Mann has published numerous articles in various law journals and has authored several legal casebooks. Seth R. Belzley is an attorney specializing in corporate finance and certain regulatory issues. He is a former managing editor of the Texas Law Review *and held a fellowship in the Center for Law, Business, and Economics. He has published several academic papers concerning the Internet.*

The Internet has become part of our daily lives, for work, education, and recreation. Online criminal activity has grown along with legitimate Internet applications. Because the Internet is a global network, it has been difficult for law enforcement agencies to effectively police online activity. Government should devise regulations that can be applied across law-enforcement jurisdictions and national boundaries, in order to make the Internet more secure.

Although the Internet undeniably has brought increased efficiency to American firms, eased communication among distant friends, and changed how we shop, book travel arrangements, and provide and enjoy entertainment, it also af-

Ronald J. Mann and Seth R. Belzley, "The Promise of Internet Intermediary Liability," *William and Mary Law Review*, vol. 47:1, October 2005, pp. 239–308.

fords the same ease of communication, increased efficiency, and, importantly, anonymity for those who prefer to use those advantages to violate the law. Legal reactions to one pervasive violation, the Internet-based piracy of copyrighted works, have been especially vigorous, perhaps because that activity poses a serious threat to an entrenched industry scared of losing its grasp over its only asset—copyrighted works. Countless numbers of reporter and law review pages have been devoted to finding ways to prevent Internet piracy. Nevertheless, Internet piracy continues and promises to recover from its recent dip, as software developers and users adapt and evolve to avoid the legal regime's current attempts to control their activities. . . .

A number of the Internet's other common uses for unlawful purposes . . . have attracted much less attention. For example, each day gamblers physically present in jurisdictions that outlaw gambling bet millions of dollars on card games and sports matches. Although Internet use arguably does not affect the illegality of that gambling, little has been done to curtail the activity. Further, the Internet has made the balance between regulating socially unacceptable forms of speech and violating the First Amendment more difficult, leading to the proliferation of material such as child pornography. Similarly, the anonymity that the Internet fosters has made it easier to buy and sell counterfeit goods, pharmaceuticals that are not lawfully available in the jurisdiction of purchase, and other forms of contraband. Moreover, Americans spend billions of dollars and millions of hours each year combating computer viruses spread over the Internet.

Service Providers and Online Companies

Although the Internet has improved our lives in dozens of ways, it has also given rise to detrimental behavior that has proven hard to constrain. Controlling that conduct without restraining the Internet's potential is surely a worthy goal. . . .

The impulse to respond to those problems inevitably involves ISPs [Internet service providers] and other Internet intermediaries, chiefly payment intermediaries (PIs), such as PayPal, and auction intermediaries, such as eBay. . . . The Internet's rise presents regulators with new challenges by making it easier for illicit actors to conceal their identities and to locate themselves in jurisdictions beyond the reach or influence of U.S. law enforcement officials.

Meanwhile, Internet intermediaries often play critical roles in the illicit behavior that frustrates regulators. Indeed, Internet intermediaries often profit directly from transactions that effectively would be banned in an offline environment. Of course, policymakers have not been blind to the possibility of employing Internet intermediaries to control their customers' misconduct. As early as 1995, a task force created by President [Bill] Clinton suggested imposing strict liability on ISPs as a means for controlling some of the Internet's dangers. More recently, state attorneys general and the Bureau of Alcohol, Tobacco, Firearms, and Explosives (ATF) reached an agreement with major credit card companies to prevent the processing of payments for illegal Internet cigarette sales. Similar initiatives have been proposed in Congress to address the problem of online sales of prescription drugs, and Pennsylvania passed a statute that but for being held unconstitutional would have required ISPs to block access to child pornography sites. Private parties have pursued intermediaries under principles of tort law. For example, in recent suits against [software company] Grokster and eBay, plaintiffs have directed their attention to Internet intermediaries in trying to curtail conduct that has detrimental effects on their businesses.

Thus far, however, the law has failed to respond in a way that effectively regulates the activity of the intermediaries. On the contrary, as discussed above, to the extent that Congress has addressed the question, it has designed laws to insulate the intermediaries from liability. State regulators have been considerably more aggressive, but . . . much of the existing formal legislative activity has either fallen in the face of litigation or has encountered problems with coordinating efforts among multiple jurisdictions. . . .

The time has come for the Internet to grow up and for Congress and the businesses that rely on the Internet to accept a mature scheme of regulation that limits the social costs of illegal Internet conduct in the most cost-effective manner. . . .

The Internet's Structure Contributes to Crime

The Internet is essentially a series of computers connected through a complex system of cables. Originally, the United States Government conceived of and designed the Internet for use by the military and university researchers. When use of the Internet was confined exclusively to the military, military contractors, university researchers, or the military itself managed connections between computers. But as the Internet was adapted to public use, private companies emerged to provide the links among private computers connected to the Internet.

The pirates have arrived on the high seas of the online world and the lack of regulation makes their predations all too easy.

Today, the Internet is a web of privately owned networks that communicate using a common computer language called Transfer Control Protocol/Internet Protocol (TCP/IP). When an Internet user requests data over the Internet, the user's request is routed first from the user's computer to the network to which the computer is connected, then across lines to the network that the computer holding the requested content is connected to, and finally to the computer that contains the requested content. These separate networks that comprise the Internet could be operated using a number of different transfer languages. The Internet's structure and the common use of TCP/IP for transfer between networks allow these different networks to communicate with each other. . . .

The basic problem with regulating content in an Internet era is that content can reside on any computer in the world that can be connected to the Internet. Thus, regulations that prohibit the dissemination of particular content often cannot reach those that make content available in places where it is unlawful. A policymaker could respond to that situation in a number of ways: by accepting a status quo in which laws on the books tacitly are flouted by widespread Internet conduct, by formalizing the futility of regulation by abandoning the regulations entirely, or by adopting a new system of regulation that is more effective. . . .

Time for Government Action

The Internet is coming of age. Though at the Internet's advent it may have been necessary to develop laws and policies that protected the fertile ground in which the businesses and technologies of the Internet have grown, today the Internet has taken hold and permeates our daily lives. Virtually every U.S. company of any significant size, even those whose core business is entirely unrelated to the Internet, has incorporated the Internet into its business model to increase efficiency and customer service. At the same time, however, harm perpetrated over the Internet continues to grow each year. The pirates have arrived on the high seas of the online world and the lack of regulation makes their predations all too easy. The time has come for lawmakers to implement sensible policies designed to reign in the pirates while minimizing the impact on law-abiding Internet users.

As the Internet enters the final stage in its development, lawmakers [should] carefully reconsider the early policy of Congress that Internet intermediaries should not bear any burden in bringing order to the Internet. This policy ignores an essential truth of the online world, namely that anonymity and porous international borders make targeting primary [offenders] difficult, if not impossible. Internet intermediaries, on the other hand, are easy to identify and have permanent commercial roots inside the jurisdictions that seek to regulate the Internet. Further, these Internet intermediaries are essential to most of the transactions on which the Internet pirates rely. When intermediaries have the technological capability to prevent harmful transactions and when the costs of doing so are reasonable in relation to the harm prevented, they should be encouraged to do so, with the threat of formal legal sanction if necessary.

The Internet is indeed at a crossroads in its development. Whether pirates will continue to threaten legitimate users of the Internet or instead whether the Internet will fulfill its potential for helping users live more fulfilling lives depends on the direction lawmakers take in facing the challenges that currently befall the Internet. Existing businesses that derive large profits from the misconduct, for example, payment intermediaries with respect to child pornography, may resist reforms vigorously. Conversely, market forces or informal pressure applied from state regulatory officials may solve many problems without the need for specific legislative intervention. Alternatively, continuing market pressures may force improved standards of operation that will solve many of the problems.

4

Government Should Not Regulate the Internet

Michael R. Nelson

Michael R. Nelson is the director of Internet technology and strategy at IBM Corporation and also serves as vice president for policy of the Internet Society. He was formerly the director of technology policy at the Federal Communications Commission.

The Internet is currently governed by various international nonprofit, nongovernmental organizations. These organizations do a good job of governing the Internet, although improvements are needed. Any changes to Internet governance should be made by these organizations, and governments should not get involved in regulating the Internet. Governments already have influence over the Internet because they regulate business operations within their jurisdictions. Governmental control of the Internet would limit the growth and usefulness of the Internet as a tool for worldwide communication.

Now that the Internet has become a keystone of global communications and commerce, many individuals and institutions are racing to jump in front of the parade and take over its governance. In the tradition of all those short-sighted visionaries who would kill the goose who lays the golden eggs, they seem unable to understand that one reason for the Internet's success is its unique governance structure. Built on the run and still evolving, the Internet governance system is a

Michael R. Nelson, "Let the Internet Be the Internet," *Issues in Science and Technology*, vol. 22.3, spring 2006, pp. 36–39. Copyright 2006 by the University of Texas at Dallas, Richardson, TX. Reprinted with permission.

hearty hybrid of technical task forces, Website operators, professional societies, information technology companies, and individual users that has somehow helped to guide the growth of an enormous, creative, flexible, and immensely popular communications system. What the Internet does not need is a government-directed top-down bureaucracy that is likely to stifle its creativity.

The call to "improve" Internet governance was heard often at the United Nations (UN)-organized November 2005 World Summit on the Information Society (WSIS) in Tunis [Tunisia], which was a followup to the December 2003 summit in Geneva [Switzerland]. Although many different topics were on the agenda in Geneva and Tunis, by far the largest amount of controversy (and press coverage) was generated by debates over Internet governance. The summit participants had very different ideas about how the Internet should be managed and who should influence its development. Many governments were uncomfortable with the status quo, in which the private companies actually building and running the Internet have the lead role. One hot-button issue was the management of domain names, which today is overseen by the International Corporation for Assigned Names and Numbers (ICANN), an internationally organized nonprofit corporation. A number of countries feel that the U.S. government exerts too much control over ICANN through a memorandum of understanding between ICANN and the U.S. Department of Commerce. As a result, a number of proposals were put forward to give governments and intergovernmental organizations, such as the UN, more control over the domain-name system.

Who Controls the Internet?

But the debate over ICANN was just part of a much bigger debate over who controls the Internet and the content that flows over it. At the Geneva Summit, a UN Working Group on Internet Governance (WGIG) was created to examine the full range of issues related to management of the Internet, which it defined as "the development and application by governments, the private sector and civil society, in their respective roles, of shared principles, norms, rules, decision-making procedures, and programmes that shape the evolution and use of the Internet."

This definition would include the standards process at organizations such as the Internet Engineering Task Force (IETF), the International Telecommunication Union (ITU), and the World Wide Web Consortium (W3C), as well as dozens of other groups; the work of ICANN and the regional Internet registries that allocate Internet protocol addresses; the spectrum-allocation decisions regarding WiFi and WiMax wireless Internet technologies; trade rules regarding e-commerce set by the World Trade Organization; procedures of international groups of law enforcement agencies for fighting cybercrime; agreements among Internet service providers (ISPs) regarding how they share Internet traffic; and efforts by multilateral organizations such as the World Bank to support the development of the Internet in less developed countries. . . .

The main reason why the Internet has grown so rapidly and why so many powerful applications can run on it is because the Internet was designed to provide individual users with as many choices and as much flexibility as possible, while preserving the end-to-end nature of the network. And the amount of choice and flexibility continues to increase. Because there are competing groups with competing solutions to users' problems, users, vendors, and providers get to determine how the Internet evolves. The genius of the Internet is that open standards and open processes enable anyone with a good idea to develop, propose, and promote new standards and applications.

The governance of the Internet has been fundamentally different from that of older telecommunications infrastructures. Until 20 to 30 years ago, governance of the international telephone system was quite simple and straightforward. Governments were in charge. In most countries, they either ran or owned the monopoly national telephone company. Telephone users were called "subscribers," because like magazine subscribers they subscribed to the service offered at the price offered and did not have much opportunity to customize their services. When governments needed to cooperate or coordinate on issues related to international telephone links, they worked through the ITU.

Governments already have a powerful influence on the market because they are large, important customers.

How Is the Internet Governed?

The model for Internet governance is completely different. At each level, there are many actors, often competing with each other. As a result, users—not governments and phone companies—have the most influence. Hundreds of millions of Internet users around the world make individual decisions every day, about which ISP to use, which browser to use, which operating systems to use, and which Internet applications and Web pages to use. Those individual decisions determine which of the offerings provided by thousands of ISPs, software companies, and hardware manufacturers succeed in the marketplace and thus determine how the Internet develops. Users' demands drive innovation and competition. Governments already have a powerful influence on the market because they are large, important customers and because they define the regulatory environment in which companies operate. Because the Internet is truly global, there is a need for coordination on a range of issues, including Internet standards, the management of domain names, cybercrime, and spectrum allocation. But these different tasks are not and cannot be handled by a single organization, because so many different players are involved. Another difference is that unlike the telephony model, where a large number of telephony-related topics (such as telephone technical standards, the assignment of telephone country codes, and the allocation of cellular frequencies) are handled by the ITU, an intergovernmental organization, most international Internet issues are dealt with by nongovernmental bodies, which in some cases are competing with each other.

In many ways, the debate over ICANN and the role of governments in the allocation of domain names can be seen as a debate between these two different models of governance: the top-down telephony model and the bottom-up Internet model. In the old telephony model, the ITU, and particularly the government members of the ITU, determined the country codes for international phone calls, set the accounting rates that fixed the cost of international phone calls, and oversaw the setting of standards for telephone equipment. National governments set telecommunications policies, which had a huge impact on the local market for telephone services and on who could provide international phone service.

Today, Internet governance covers a wider range of issues, and for most of these issues the private sector, not governments, have the lead role. In contrast to telephony standards, which are set by the ITU, Internet standards are set by the Internet Engineering Task Force, the World Wide Web Consortium, and dozens of other private-sector-led organizations, as well as more informal consortia of information technology companies. However, some members of the ITU, as part of its Next Generation Networks initiative, are suggesting that the ITU needs to develop new standards to replace those developed at the IETF and elsewhere.

Likewise, the ITU is not content to have the price of international Internet connections determined by the market. For more than seven years, an ITU working group has been exploring ways in which the old accounting rates model for telephony might be adapted and applied to the Internet. Ironically, the ITU pricing mechanism has already had an effect on the Internet. Exorbitant international phone rates, which can be more than a dollar per minute in some countries, have given a big boost to the use of voice over Internet protocol (VOIP) services, which allow computer users to make phone calls without paying per-minute fees. During the time that the ITU has been discussing ways to regulate the cost of international Internet connection, in most markets the cost of international broadband links has plummeted by 90 to 95%. This apparently was not good enough for many WSIS participants, who insisted that regulation was needed to bring down user costs.

What Needs to Be Governed Online?

WSIS participants also offered a number of proposals to have governments and the ITU take a larger role in regulating the applications that run over the Internet. For instance, several governments called for regulatory action to fight spam and digital piracy, protect online privacy, enhance consumer protection, and improve cybersecurity. Of course, Internet users and managers are addressing all these issues in a variety of ways, and a robust market exists for security tools and services. As a result, users have many options from which to select what works best for them. In contrast, some governments are talking about the need for comprehensive, one-size-fits-all solutions to spam, digital rights management, or cybercrime. Imposing this kind of rigid top-down solution on the Internet would have the undesirable side effect of "freezing in" current technological fixes and hindering the development of more powerful new tools and applications. Even more disturbing, in many cases the cure would be worse than the disease, because solutions proposed to limit spam or fraudulent content could also be used by governments to censor citizens' access to politically sensitive information.

The debate over Internet governance is really about the future direction of the Internet. One outcome of the Tunis Summit was the creation of the Internet Governance Forum (IGF), a multistakeholder discussion group that will examine how decisions about the future of the Internet are made. Those advocating a greater role for governments in managing the Internet will continue to press their case at the IGF. The debate over ICANN will provide the first indication of where the discussion is heading. If a large majority of governments decide that ICANN should be replaced by an intergovernmental body or that government should have more say in ICANN decision-making, we can expect to hear more calls for greater government regulation in a wide range of areas, from Internet pricing to content control to Internet standards.

The existing Internet governance structure has repeatedly demonstrated its capacity to solve problems as they arise.

Fortunately, the Tunis Summit also exposed many government leaders to a broader understanding of how the Internet is governed and how it can contribute to the well-being of people throughout the world. They learned that the ICANN squabble is a relatively minor concern among the challenges that confront the Internet. The farmer in central Africa, the teacher in the Andes, or the small merchant in Central Asia does not care about where ICANN is incorporated or how it is structured. But they care about the cost of access and whether they can get technical advice on how to connect to and use the Internet. They care about whether the Internet is secure and reliable. They care about whether there are useful Internet content and services in their native language. And in many countries, they care about whether they'll be thrown in jail for something they write in a chat room.

Who Should Control the Internet?

As the national governments, companies, nongovernmental organizations, and others involved in WSIS work to achieve the goals agreed to in Tunis, they should use the organizations that are already shaping the way the Internet is run. The existing Internet governance structure has repeatedly demonstrated its capacity to solve problems as they arise. Rather than discarding what has proven successful, world leaders should be trying to understand how it has succeeded, explaining this process to stakeholders and the public so that they can be more effective in participating in the process, and using the lessons of the past in approaching new problems. For instance, the IETF has set many of the fundamental standards of the Internet, and it is in the best position to build on those standards to continue improving Internet performance. As more people want to participate in standard setting, the IETF needs to explain to the new arrivals how it operates. To help in this effort, the Internet Society has started a newsletter to help make the IETF process more accessible and to invite input from an even larger community. The IETF is open to all. It is not even necessary to come to the three meetings that the IETF holds each year, because much of the work is done online.

Other Internet-related groups are also eager to find ways to ensure that their work and its implications are understood and supported by the broadest possible community. They should follow the IETF example by making standards and publications available for free online and by publishing explanations of what they do in lay language. They could convene online forums where critical issues are discussed and where individuals and government representatives could express their views. As part of the preparation for the June 2005 World Urban Forum in Vancouver [Canada], the UN staged HabitatJam, a three-day online forum that attracted 39,000 participants. It could certainly do the same for Internet issues.

Ten or 15 years ago, when the Internet was still mostly the domain of researchers and academics, it was possible to bring together in a single meeting most of the key decisionmakers working on Internet standards and technology as well as the people who cared about their implications. That is no longer possible, except by using the Internet itself. The Internet Society is already starting to reach out to other organizations to explore how such public events could be organized.

The Current System Is Working

Before trying to reinvent Internet governance, those who are unhappy with some Internet practices or who see untapped potential for Internet expansion should begin by using the mechanisms that have proved effective for the past two decades. The Internet continues to grow at an amazing pace, new applications are being developed daily, and new business models are being tried. The current system encourages experimentation and innovation. The Internet has grown and prospered as a bottom-up system. A top-down governance system would alter its very essence. Instead, all who care about the Internet need to work together to find ways to strengthen the bottom-up model that has served the Internet and the Internet community so well.

Two years ago, at a meeting of the UN Information and Communication Technologies Task Force in New York, Vint Cerf, the chairman of ICANN, said, "If it ain't broke, don't fix it." Some people have misinterpreted his words to mean that nothing is wrong and nothing needs to be fixed. No one believes that. We have many issues to address. We need to reduce the cost of Internet access and connect the unconnected; we need to improve the security of cyberspace and fight spam; we need to make it easier to support non-Latin alphabets; we need to promote the adoption of new standards that will enable new, innovative uses of the Internet; and we need better ways of fighting and stopping cybercriminals.

The good news is that we have many different institutions collaborating (and sometimes competing) to find ways to address these problems. Many of those institutions—from the IETF to ICANN to the ITU—are adapting and reaching out to constituencies that were not part of the process in the past. They are becoming more open and transparent. That is helpful and healthy, but we need to continue to strive to make it better. In particular, it would be very useful if funding could be found so that the most talented engineers from the developing world could take more of a role in the Internet rulemaking bodies, so that the concerns of Internet users in those countries could be factored into the technical decisions being made there.

The debate about the future of the Internet should not begin with who gets the impressive titles and who travels to the big meetings. It should begin with the individual Internet user and the individual who has not yet been able to connect. It should focus on the issues that will affect their lives and the way they use the Internet. Most of them do not want a seat on the standards committees. They want to have choice in how they connect to the Internet and the power to use this powerful enabling technology in the ways that best suit their needs and conditions.

5

Cyberterrorism Is a Serious Threat

John Mallery

John Mallery is a computer forensics specialist in Kansas City, Missouri. He is a contributing editor of Security Technology and Design *magazine and cowrote the book* Hardening Network Security.

Many people do not believe that cyberterrorism is a serious threat to the security of the United States. It is easy to imagine scenarios of large-scale terrorist acts directly or indirectly involving the Internet. There are a number of ways in which terrorists could use the Internet to their benefit, and in most cases it would be relatively easy to do so. A cyberterrorism attack on the United States is inevitable. Governments and emergency response agencies should increase security and preparedness to guard against cyberterrorism.

Pundits, the media, security directors and politicians disagree on the significance of the cyberterrorism threat. Immediately after 9/11 [the September 11, 2001 attacks on America], the public media and the industry seemed to consider it a high-stakes issue, but as time passed the tone of most articles reflected that the threat was being blown out of proportion.

It's not surprising there's no consensus, considering that many people don't even have a clear understanding of the

John Mallery, "Cyberterrorism: Real Threat or Media Hype?" *Security Technology and Design*, vol. 22.3, May 2005, pp. 58, 60, 62, 64.

term cyberterrorism. It refers to a politically motivated, computer-based attack that is designed to cause a catastrophic event resulting in physical harm, death and fear among a large population base.

Individuals have proposed numerous cyberterror scenarios, such as hacking into the control systems of a hydroelectric dam and releasing a flood on downstream communities, and hacking into air traffic control systems to cause the crash of a passenger jet. Are these real threats, or is the cyberterrorist just another bogeyman?

Is the Threat Overblown?

I have several friends who are cybercrime investigators for various law enforcement agencies. I conducted an informal survey with the promise of anonymity, asking if any of them was aware of true cyberterrorist attacks or investigations. They were all aware of numerous hacking attacks, but none were aware of any cyberterrorist attacks or investigations. This lends some credibility to the belief that the cyberterrorist threat has been blown out of proportion.

It appears that terrorists are not only knocking on the door of our infrastructure, they're pounding on it with hinge-shaking force.

Industries may have proactively implemented practices to minimize such attacks. For instance, many have realized that interconnectivity, although convenient, is not necessarily a good idea. In the recently released U.S. Nuclear Regulatory Commission Draft Regulatory Guide DG-1130, "Criteria for Use of Computers in Safety Systems of Nuclear Power Plants," remote connectivity is directly addressed.

The draft states: "Remote access to the safety system software functions or data from outside the technical environment of the plant (e.g., from the administrative or engineering buildings or from outside the plant) that involves a potential security threat to safety functions should not be implemented."

It should be noted that adherence to these guidelines is strictly voluntary. Still, even when critical infrastructure facilities are connected, they tend to be extremely difficult to get into. Hacking into the control center of a water treatment plant or power company requires a great deal more sophistication and expertise than hacking into a system to download R&D [research and development] documents or credit card numbers.

Staying on Guard

Even though cyberterrorism appears to be a non-event, I think it is dangerous to let our guard down. Determined terrorists are still trying to find ways into the systems controlling our infrastructure, and they will keep knocking at the door in hopes that someday they can get in.

In a recent presentation, the security director of a large Midwestern utility company provided statistics showing the hits on the company's firewalls from unfriendly foreign nations. The numbers were staggering. It appears that terrorists are not only knocking on the door of our infrastructure, they're pounding on it with hinge-shaking force. Sooner or later, they will break through, either as the result of a system malfunction or new knowledge and expertise that will allow them to bypass current security mechanisms.

In addition, despite the warnings, many organizations are throwing wide the door because they find the convenience of interconnectivity too alluring to ignore. Not only are they embracing the convenience of standard networking technologies, but they are even embracing the newer wireless technologies. I believe it is only a matter of time before a true cyberterrorism attack occurs within the United States.

Don't Underestimate the Enemy

Perhaps the individuals who minimize the cyberterrorism threat underestimate the skill sets of our enemies. It is already understood that terrorists use computers on a regular basis for communication and research.

In January of 2003, [U.S. secretary of defense] Donald Rumsfeld quoted from a recovered al Qaeda training manual: "Using public sources openly and without resorting to illegal means, it is possible to gather at least 80 percent of all information required about the enemy." Much of this information can be found on the Internet.

Even if information on a target is not directly available on the Internet, a little digging can usually uncover the information required. To illustrate this, I ran an online search for information on the only nuclear power plant in Kansas, which provides more than 23 percent of the energy needs for the state.

The greater the fear, the greater the disruption.

This facility has a wonderful Web site describing the power plant and its history, and offering excellent nuclear energy information. There is no map to the facility, and no street address is provided for either the power plant or a corporate office. However, a simple Whois.com search for the Web site's domain name provides a street address.

Of course, it is a far cry from surfing the Internet for information to hacking into the control system. But it is important to recognize that many terrorists are extremely intelligent and have many resources. If they cannot find the information they need on the Internet, they can purchase it. If they require training on a particular piece of software, they can purchase the software and the training.

We all recognize that insiders, as well as former employees, pose a threat to our information today. It is not far-fetched that terrorists could purchase information or knowledge from these same people.

In 2000, Vitek Boden, a former employee of an Australian wastewater services provider, used his expertise to take remote control of a sewage treatment plant in Australia and released nearly 300 thousand gallons of raw sewage into waterways. This in and of itself is frightening, but the fact that it took him 45 attempts before he was finally successful is the key point. No one noticed his previous 44 attempts! How many other utilities are under attack that no one is aware of?

Coordinated Attacks

Although I believe cyberterrorism is a threat, what really concerns me is what I call "one off" cyberterrorism—the use of technology to maximize the impact of a more standard terrorist attack. One of the goals of a terrorist attack is to cause fear in the target population, since fear often changes behavior patterns, which in turn can disrupt an economy. The greater the fear, the greater the disruption.

It is important to recognize that most disaster management and disaster response plans are stored on networked computers for ease of access. These plans often outline how a community will respond to a particular attack or threat, including which agencies or departments are designated as first responders. If terrorists wanted to maximize the impact of an attack such as the release of a biological agent or the detonation of a dirty bomb, they would do everything in their power to impede the ability of the first responders to address the attack.

Preventing ambulances, firefighters and police from promptly arriving on the scene could cause the death toll to rise and could allow toxic agents to spread over a wider area.

Hacking into the systems storing these disaster management plans would provide all the information necessary to accomplish this.

Many cities list the addresses of all fire stations. This can help terrorists locate the appropriate stations to impede via an additional bomb or attack. Other systems that could be targets include law enforcement's computer-aided dispatch systems.

These systems are often integrated with GPS [Global Positioning System] so that the exact location of patrol cars can be determined. I believe these systems will become more vulnerable as agencies add functionally to them. Many are linked to other agencies in an effort to quickly share relevant information. The more interconnectivity added the greater the risk of attack.

These risks are only compounded by the fact that many law enforcement agencies do not have the resources—funds or staffing—to adequately monitor their networks for intrusions. Theoretically, terrorists could have already compromised many of these systems.

Other information that is stored on computers that may be of interest to terrorists includes:

- Routes for vehicles transporting hazardous waste
- Locations of power plants
- Locations of fuel supplies for municipalities
- Storage areas for grain, cattle and other agricultural products
- Locations of communications centers
- Purchase history for first responders—identifying equipment available to public safety professionals
- Storage locations of dangerous chemicals

- Road construction plans
- Scheduling of security teams for special events
- Locations of power lines, water lines and gas lines
- Date, time and location of special events (large gatherings of people)

A Well Planned Attack

With the information listed above terrorists could perpetrate a well planned and devastating attack on, for instance, a large public event.

- If terrorists can find information that indicates whether the security team sheduled to cover the event intends to search for explosives, they can plan a suicide bombing around that information. If there is to be no searching, they may use a stable, traditional explosive. If there is going to be searching, they may choose an explosive that is less stable, but easy to make and much more difficult to detect. Having prior knowledge of what types of explosives can get past security mechanisms increases the probability of success.
- If they can find out what types of toxic gases the local first responders are ill equipped to address—something that may be evident from first responder purchase histories—terrorists may plan to release one of those gases into the crowd.
- With the addresses of the local fire stations and hospitals, terrorists may be able to impede first responders' attempts to reach the site of the event. They may create an accident in front of a fire station, drop a large amount of spikes in front of an ambulance facility to puncture tires, or pour Karo [corn] syrup into the fuel tanks of MedEvac helicopters to slow down response times.

- Since most communication systems are now computer based, terrorists could use automated programs to flood communications systems, again increasing the impact of the attack by confusing attempts to mitigate the damage.

All of these things could be accomplished by hacking into networked systems that are often less protected than the control systems for our infrastructure.

This type of one-off cyberterrorist attack is more of a reality than direct cyberterrorism, and it has a greater likelihood of success. Because of this, every government entity tasked with emergency preparedness should have line items in their budgets for protecting their computer systems and networks. If they don't, the emergencies they are preparing for could be much worse than expected.

6

Cyberterrorism Is Not a Serious Threat

Joshua Green

Joshua Green is an editor of the Washington Monthly. *He has also contributed to the* New Yorker, *the* New York Times, Slate, *the* American Prospect, *and the* Onion. *He was recognized as one of Columbia Journalism Review's rising young writers and was named as a finalist for the 2002 Livingston Award for Young Journalists.*

A cyberterrorist attack is unlikely. Terrorists use the Internet for communication, but the Internet cannot be used to cause widespread death and destruction. Exaggerated concern over cyberterrorism has taken attention away from real problems such as computer viruses and data theft. Government and private companies should focus on addressing these more serious computer security threats.

Again and again since September 11, [2001] President [George W.] Bush, Vice President [Dick] Cheney, and senior administration officials have alerted the public not only to the dangers of chemical, biological, and nuclear weapons but also to the further menace of cyberterrorism. "Terrorists can sit at one computer connected to one network and can create worldwide havoc," warned Homeland Security Director Tom Ridge in a representative observation [in April 2001]. "[They] don't necessarily need a bomb or explosives to cripple a sector of the economy, or shut down a power grid."

Joshua Green, "The Myth of Cyberterrorism: There Are Many Ways Terrorists Can Kill You—Computers Aren't One of Them," *Washington Monthly*, November 2002.

Even before September 11, Bush was fervently depicting an America imminently in danger of an attack by cyberterrorists, warning during his presidential campaign that "American forces are overused and underfunded precisely when they are confronted by a host of new threats and challenges—the spread of weapons of mass destruction, the rise of cyberterrorism, the proliferation of missile technology." In other words, the country is confronted not just by the specter of terrorism, but by a menacing new breed of it that is technologically advanced, little understood, and difficult to defend against. Since September 11, these concerns have only multiplied. A survey of 725 cities conducted by the National League of Cities for the anniversary of the attacks shows that cyberterrorism ranks with biological and chemical weapons atop officials' lists of fears.

Concern over cyberterrorism is particularly acute in Washington. As is often the case with a new threat, an entire industry has arisen to grapple with its ramifications—think tanks have launched new projects and issued white papers, experts have testified to its dangers before Congress, private companies have hastily deployed security consultants and software designed to protect public and private targets, and the media have trumpeted the threat with such front-page headlines as this one, in *The Washington Post* [in June 2001]: "Cyber-Attacks by Al Qaeda Feared, Terrorists at Threshold of Using Internet as Tool of Bloodshed, Experts Say."

The federal government has requested $4.5 billion for infrastructure security next year; the FBI [Federal Bureau of Investigation] boasts more than 1,000 "cyber investigators"; President Bush and Vice President Cheney keep the issue before the public; and in response to September 11, Bush created the office of "cybersecurity czar" in the White House, naming to this position Richard Clarke, who has done more than anyone to raise awareness, including warning that "if an attack comes today with information warfare . . . it would be much, much worse than Pearl Harbor."

It's no surprise, then, that cyberterrorism now ranks alongside other weapons of mass destruction in the public consciousness. Americans have had a latent fear of catastrophic computer attack ever since a teenage Matthew Broderick hacked into the Pentagon's nuclear weapons system and nearly launched World War III in the 1983 movie *WarGames*. Judging by official alarums and newspaper headlines, such scenarios are all the more likely in today's wired world.

Nuclear weapons and other sensitive military systems enjoy the most basic form of Internet security: they're "air-gapped," meaning that they're not physically connected to the Internet and are therefore inaccessible to outside hackers.

Cyberterrorism Does Not Exist

There's just one problem: There is no such thing as cyberterrorism—no instance of anyone ever having been killed by a terrorist (or anyone else) using a computer. Nor is there compelling evidence that al Qaeda or any other terrorist organization has resorted to computers for any sort of serious destructive activity. What's more, outside of a Tom Clancy novel, computer security specialists believe it is virtually impossible to use the Internet to inflict death on a large scale, and many scoff at the notion that terrorists would bother trying. "I don't lie awake at night worrying about cyberattacks ruining my life," says Dorothy Denning, a computer science professor at Georgetown University and one of the country's foremost cybersecurity experts. "Not only does [cyberterrorism] not rank alongside chemical, biological, or nuclear weapons, but it is not anywhere near as serious as other potential physical threats like car bombs or suicide bombers."

Which is not to say that cybersecurity isn't a serious problem—it's just not one that involves terrorists. Interviews with terrorism and computer security experts, and current and former government and military officials, yielded near unanimous agreement that the real danger is from the criminals and other hackers who did $15 billion in damage to the global economy last year using viruses, worms, and other readily available tools. That figure is sure to balloon if more isn't done to protect vulnerable computer systems, the vast majority of which are in the private sector. Yet when it comes to imposing the tough measures on business necessary to protect against the real cyberthreats, the Bush administration has balked.

When ordinary people imagine cyberterrorism, they tend to think along Hollywood plot lines, doomsday scenarios in which terrorists hijack nuclear weapons, airliners, or military computers from halfway around the world. Given the colorful history of federal boondoggles—billion-dollar weapons systems that misfire, $600 toilet seats—that's an understandable concern. But, with few exceptions, it's not one that applies to preparedness for a cyberattack. "The government is miles ahead of the private sector when it comes to cybersecurity," says Michael Cheek, director of intelligence for iDefense, a Virginia-based computer security company with government and private-sector clients. "Particularly the most sensitive military systems."

Serious effort and plain good fortune have combined to bring this about. Take nuclear weapons. The biggest fallacy about their vulnerability, promoted in action thrillers like *WarGames*, is that they're designed for remote operation. "[The movie] is premised on the assumption that there's a modem bank hanging on the side of the computer that controls the missiles," says Martin Libicki, a defense analyst at the RAND Corporation. "I assure you, there isn't." Rather, nuclear weapons and other sensitive military systems enjoy the most basic form of Internet security: they're "air-gapped," meaning that they're not physically connected to the Internet and are therefore inaccessible to outside hackers. (Nuclear weapons also contain "permissive action links," mechanisms to prevent weapons from being armed without inputting codes carried by the president.) A retired military official was somewhat indignant at the mere suggestion: "As a general principle, we've been looking at this thing for 20 years. What cave have you been living in if you haven't considered this [threat]?"

The Risk Is Slim

When it comes to cyberthreats, the Defense Department has been particularly vigilant to protect key systems by isolating them from the Net and even from the Pentagon's internal network. All new software must be submitted to the National Security Agency for security testing. "Terrorists could not gain control of our spacecraft, nuclear weapons, or any other type of high-consequence asset," says Air Force Chief Information Officer [CIO] John Gilligan. [In 2001] Pentagon CIO John Stenbit enforced a moratorium on new wireless networks, which are often easy to hack into, as well as common wireless devices such as PDAs [personal digital assistants], BlackBerrys, and even wireless or infrared copiers and faxes.

The September 11 hijackings led to an outcry that airliners are particularly susceptible to cyberterrorism. [In 2002] for instance, Sen. Charles Schumer (D-N.Y.) described "the absolute havoc and devastation that would result if cyberterrorists suddenly shut down our air traffic control system, with thousands of planes in mid-flight." In fact, cybersecurity experts give some of their highest marks to the FAA [Federal Aviation Administration], which reasonably separates its administrative and air traffic control systems and strictly air-gaps the latter. And there's a reason the 9/11 [September 11, 2001] hijackers used box-cutters instead of keyboards: It's impossible to hijack a plane remotely, which eliminates the possibility of a high-tech 9/11 scenario in which planes are used as weapons.

Another source of concern is terrorist infiltration of our intelligence agencies. But here, too, the risk is slim. The CIA's [Central Intelligence Agency] classified computers are also air-gapped, as is the FBI's entire computer system. "They've been paranoid about this forever," says Libicki, adding that paranoia is a sound governing principle when it comes to cybersecurity. Such concerns are manifesting themselves in broader policy terms as well. One notable characteristic of [the 2001] Quadrennial Defense Review was how strongly it focused on protecting information systems.

But certain tics in the way government agencies procure technology have also—entirely by accident—helped to keep them largely free of hackers. For years, agencies eschewed off-the-shelf products and insisted instead on developing proprietary systems, unique to their branch of government—a particularly savvy form of bureaucratic self-preservation. When, say, the Department of Agriculture succeeded in convincing Congress that it needed a specially designed system, both the agency and the contractor benefited. The software company was assured the agency's long-term business, which became dependent on its product; in turn, bureaucrats developed an expertise with the software that made them difficult to replace. This, of course, fostered colossal inefficiencies—agencies often couldn't communicate with each other, minor companies developed fiefdoms in certain agencies, and if a purveyor went bankrupt, the agency was left with no one to manage its technology. But it did provide a peculiar sort of protection: Outside a select few, no one understood these specific systems well enough to violate them. So in a sense, the famous inability of agencies like the FBI and INS [Immigration and Naturalization Service] to share information because of incompatible computer systems has yielded the inadvertent benefit of shielding them from attack.

Threats Are Not Realistic

That leaves the less-protected secondary targets—power grids, oil pipelines, dams, and water systems that don't present opportunities as nightmarish as do nuclear weapons, but nonetheless seem capable, under the wrong hands, of causing their own mass destruction. Because most of these systems are in the private sector and are not yet regarded as national security loopholes, they tend to be less secure than government and military systems. In addition, companies increasingly use the Internet to manage such processes as oil-pipeline flow and water levels in dams by means of "supervisory control and data acquisition" systems, or SCADA, which confers remote access. Most experts see possible vulnerability here, and though terrorists have never attempted to exploit it, media accounts often sensationalize the likelihood that they will.

To illustrate the supposed ease with which our enemies could subvert a dam, *The Washington Post*'s June [2001] story on al Qaeda cyberterrorism related an anecdote about a 12-year-old who hacked into the SCADA system at Arizona's Theodore Roosevelt Dam in 1998, and was, the article intimated, within mere keystrokes of unleashing millions of gallons of water upon helpless downstream communities. But a subsequent investigation by the tech-news site *CNet.com* revealed the tale to be largely apocryphal—the incident occurred in 1994, the hacker was 27, and, most importantly, investigators concluded that he couldn't have gained control of the dam and that no lives or property were ever at risk.

Most hackers break in simply for sport. To the extent that these hacks occur, they're mainly Web site defacements, which are a nuisance, but leave the intruder no closer to exploiting the system in any deadly way. Security experts dismiss such hackers as "ankle biters" and roll their eyes at prognostications of doom.

Of course, it's conceivable that a computer-literate terrorist truly intent on wreaking havoc could hack into computers at a dam or power company. But once inside, it would be far more difficult for him to cause significant damage than most people realize. "It's not the difficulty of doing it," says RAND's Libicki. "It's the difficulty of doing it and having any real consequence." "No one explains precisely the how, whys, and wherefores of these apocalyptic scenarios," says George Smith, the editor of *Crypt Newsletter*, which covers computer security issues. "You always just get the assumption that chemical plants can be made to explode, that the water supply can be polluted—things that are even hard to do physically are suddenly assumed to be elementary because of the prominence of the Internet."

Few besides a company's own employees possess the specific technical know-how required to run a specialized SCADA system. The most commonly cited example of SCADA exploitation bears this out. [In 2000], an Australian man used an Internet connection to release a million gallons of raw sewage along Queensland's Sunshine Coast after being turned down for a government job. When police arrested him; they discovered that he'd worked for the company that designed the sewage treatment plant's control software. This is true of most serious cybersecurity breaches—they tend to come from insiders. It was Robert Hanssen's familiarity with the FBI's computer system that allowed him to exploit it despite its security. In both cases, the perpetrators weren't terrorists but rogue employees with specialized knowledge difficult, if not impossible, for outsiders to acquire—a security concern, but not one attributable to cyberterrorism.

Terrorists might, in theory, try to recruit insiders. But even if they succeeded, the degree of damage they could cause would still be limited. Most worst-case scenarios (particularly those put forth by government) presuppose that no human beings are keeping watch to intervene if something goes wrong. But especially in the case of electrical power grids, oil and gas utilities, and communications companies, this is simply untrue. Such systems get hit all the time by hurricanes, floods, or tornadoes, and company employees are well rehearsed in handling the fallout. This is equally true when the trouble stems from human action. [In 2000] in California, energy companies like Enron and El Paso Corp. conspired to cause power shortages that led to brownouts and blackouts—the same effects cyberterrorists would wreak. As Smith points out, "There were no newspaper reports of people dying as a result of the blackouts. No one lost their mind." The state suffered only minor (if demoralizing) inconvenience.

Despite all the media alarm about terrorists poised on the verge of cyberattack, intelligence suggests that they're doing no more than emailing and surfing for potential targets.

But perhaps the best indicator of what is realistic came [in July 2002] when the U.S. Naval War College contracted with a research group to simulate a massive attack on the nation's information infrastructure. Government hackers and security analysts gathered in Newport, R.I., for a war game dubbed "Digital Pearl Harbor." The result? The hackers failed to crash the Internet, though they did cause serious sporadic damage. But, according to a *CNet.com* report, officials concluded that terrorists hoping to stage such an attack "would require a syndicate with significant resources, including $200 million, country-level intelligence and five years of preparation time."

The Internet's Role in Terror

Despite all the media alarm about terrorists poised on the verge of cyberattack, intelligence suggests that they're doing no more than emailing and surfing for potential targets. When U.S. troops recovered al Qaeda laptops in Afghanistan, officials were surprised to find its members more technologically adept than previously believed. They discovered structural and engineering software, electronic models of a dam, and information on computerized water systems, nuclear power plants, and U.S. and European stadiums. But nothing suggested they were planning cyberattacks, only that they were using the Internet to communicate and coordinate physical attacks. "There doesn't seem to be any evidence that the people we know as terrorists like to do cyberterrorism," says Libicki. Indeed, in a July report to the Senate Governmental Affairs Committee detailing the threats detected to critical infrastructure, the General Accounting Office noted "to date none of the traditional terrorist groups such as al Qaeda have used the Internet to launch a known assault on the U.S.'s infrastructure." It is much easier, and almost certainly much deadlier, to strike the old-fashioned way.

Government computers have been targeted by politically minded hackers, but these attacks are hardly life threatening. They're typified by [the October 2001] penetration of a Defense Department Web site dedicated to "Operation Enduring Freedom" and, somewhat incongruously, a Web server operated by the National Oceanic and Atmospheric Association. The organization responsible was called the "al Qaeda Alliance Online" and was comprised of groups with names like GForce Pakistan and the Pakistani Hackerz Club—names that connote a certain adolescent worship of hip-hop that's a clue to the participants' relative lack of menace; none turned out to have actual terrorist ties.

In both cases, the attackers replaced the government sites' home pages with photos and anti-American text—but that's all they did. Robbed of this context, as is usually the case with reports of politically motivated cyberattacks, such manifestations are often presumed to be much more serious terrorist threats than is warranted. "When somebody defaces a Web site, it's roughly equivalent to spray painting something rude on the outside of a building," says James Lewis, director of technology policy at the Center for Strategic and International Studies. "It's really just electronic graffiti."

Threats Are Exaggerated

Yet Washington hypes cyberterrorism incessantly. "Cyberterrorism and cyberattacks are sexy right now. It's novel, original, it captures people's imagination," says Georgetown's Denning. Indeed, a peculiar sort of one-upmanship has developed when describing the severity of the threat. The most popular term, "electronic Pearl Harbor," was coined in 1991 by an alarmist tech writer named Winn Schwartau to hype a novel. For a while, in the mid-1990s, "electronic Chernobyl" was in vogue. Earlier this year, Sen. Charles Schumer (D-N.Y.) warned of a looming "digital Armageddon." And the Center for Strategic and International Studies, a Washington think tank, has christened its own term, "digital Waterloo."

Why all this brooding over so relatively minor a threat? Ignorance is one reason. Cyberterrorism merges two spheres—terrorism and technology—that most lawmakers and senior administration officials don't fully understand and therefore tend to fear, making them likelier to accede to any measure, if only out of self-preservation. Just as tellingly, many are eager to exploit this ignorance. Numerous technology companies, still reeling from the collapse of the tech bubble, have recast themselves as innovators crucial to national security and boosted their Washington presence in an effort to attract federal dollars. As Ohio State University law professor Peter Swim explained to *Mother Jones*, "Many companies that rode the dot-com boom need to find big new sources of income. One is direct sales to the federal government; another is federal mandates. If we have a big federal push for new security spending, that could prop up the sagging market."

But lately, a third motive has emerged: Stoking fears of cyberterrorism helps maintain the level of public anxiety about terrorism generally, which in turn makes it easier for the administration to pass its agenda.

At the center of all this hype is Richard Clarke, special adviser to the president for cyberspace security, a veteran of four administrations, and terrorism czar to [former president] Bill Clinton. Even though he was a senior Clinton official, Clarke's legendary bureaucratic skills saw him through the transition; and when replaced by Gen. Wayne Downing after September 11, Clarke created for himself the position of cybersecurity czar and continued heralding the threat of cyberattack. Understanding that in Washington attention leads to resources and power, Clarke quickly raised the issue's profile. "Dick has an ability to scare the bejesus out of everybody and to make the bureaucracy jump," says a former colleague. The Bush administration requested a 64 percent increase in cybersecurity funds for [2003].

We've never seen any of the officially designated terrorist groups engage in a cyberattack against us.

I paid Clarke a visit in his office a few blocks west of the White House to talk about the threat and discovered that even he is beginning to wilt under the false pretense of cyberterrorism. As I was led back to meet him, his assistant made an odd request: "Mr. Clarke doesn't like to talk about the source of the threat, he'd rather focus on the vulnerability." And indeed, the man who figured most prominently in hyping the issue seemed particularly ill at ease discussing it.

Real Threats Are Elsewhere

Clarke is in the curious bind of an expert on terrorism charged to protect the nation against a form of the disease that has yet to appear. But he is smart enough to understand that one very real cybersecurity threat is unfolding: the damage, largely economic, being done by hackers and criminals. Last year, 52,000 cyberattacks were reported, up from 21,000 the year before. Yet Clarke's greatest leverage is misperception about the true source of this threat. In his careful way, he tried to guide our conversation away from terrorism and toward cybersecurity.

"To date," he readily conceded, "we've never seen any of the officially designated terrorist groups engage in a cyberattack against us." But he stressed that little noticed in the aftermath of September 11 was a large-scale cyberattack seven days later—the Nimda virus—that proved extremely costly to private industry. "Nimda hit a lot of businesses that thought they had done a good job securing themselves," Clarke explained. "And a lot of CEOs got really pissed because they thought they had spent a lot of time and money doing cybersecurity for the company and—bang!—they got hammered, knocked offline, their records got destroyed, and it cost millions of dollars per company." The $15 billion in damage caused by cyberattacks last year is derived mostly from worms, viruses, denial-of-service attacks, and theft, all of which capitalized on the generally lax cybersecurity in the private-sector businesses that comprise about 85 percent of the Internet. Many vulnerabilities are imported through the use of products by private companies, such as Microsoft, that supply software. There is no regulatory mechanism to ensure that they meet security standards; and as Clarke notes, "there's no legal liability if you are the software manufacturer and sell somebody something that doesn't work."

He also pointed out that a typical company devotes one-quarter of 1 percent of its information technology budget to cybersecurity, "slightly less than they spend on coffee." By contrast, the Bush administration's FY [fiscal year] 2003 budget would spend 8 percent, or 32 times higher a proportion. Yet even this considerable outlay doesn't guarantee that the government's systems are secure. The same poorly written and configured software that plagues private industry also hampers government computers—the federal government is, after all, Microsoft's largest customer. John Gilligan, the Air Force CIO and one of the fiercest advocates of stronger safety standards in government, says that 80 percent of successful penetrations of federal computer systems can be attributed to software full of bugs, trapdoors, and "Easter eggs"—programming errors and quirks inserted into the code that could leave software vulnerable to hackers. What's more, as federal agencies move away from proprietary systems toward universal software, this becomes a greater problem not just in terms of security, but also of cost. "The assessment I make is that we're fast approaching the point at which we're spending more money to find, patch, and correct vulnerabilities than we paid for the software," says Gilligan.

Government Has the Wrong Focus

The danger of hyping a threat like cyberterrorism is that once the exaggeration becomes clear, the public will grow cynical toward warnings about real threats. The Chicken Little approach might be excusable were the Bush administration hyping cyberterrorism in order to build political momentum for dealing with the true problem posed by hackers and shoddy software. There is a precedent for this sort of thing. In the midst of all the anxiety about the Y2K bug, the federal government and the SEC [Securities and Exchange Commission] came up with a novel way to ensure that private companies were ready: They required businesses to disclose their preparations to shareholders, setting goals and letting market forces do the rest.

There were high hopes, then, for the Bush administration's National Strategy to Secure Cyberspace—the culmination of a year's effort to address the country's post-9/11 cybersecurity problems. Clarke's team circulated early drafts that contained what most experts considered to be solid measures for shoring up security in government, business, and home computers. But the business community got word that the plan contained tough (read: potentially costly) prescriptions, and petitioned the White House, which gutted them. When a draft of the plan was rolled out in mid-September, Bill Conner, president of the computer security firm Entrust, told *The Washington Post*, "It looks as though a Ph.D. wrote the government items, but it reads like someone a year out of grade school wrote the rest of the plan."

It's hard to imagine a worse outcome for all involved, even private industry. By knuckling under to the business community's anti-regulatory impulses, Bush produced a weak plan that ultimately leaves the problem of cybersecurity to persist. It proposes no regulations, no legislation, and stops well short of even the Y2K approach, prompting most security experts to dismiss it out of hand. What it does do instead is continue the stream of officially sanctioned scaremongering about cyberattack, much to the delight of software companies. IT [information technology] security remains one of the few bright spots in the depressed tech market and thus that important sector of the market is perfectly satisfied with the status quo. But as the Nimda virus proved, even companies that pay for security software (and oppose government standards) don't realize just how poorly it protects them. So in effect, the Bush administration has created the conditions for what amounts to war profiteering—frightening businesses into investing in security, but refusing to force the changes necessary to make software safe and effective. . . . Hyping a threat that doesn't exist while shrinking from one that does is no way to protect the country.

7

Identity Theft Is a Growing Problem

Sunil Dutta

Sunil Dutta is a sergeant and crisis negotiator with the Los Angeles police department. He is a frequent contributor to various publications, including the Los Angeles Times *and* American Police Beat *and the American Civil Rights Coalition Web site.*

Identity theft is a serious crime that is growing quickly. It is fairly easy for identity theft to occur, because personal information is readily available through a variety of channels. Identity theft is costly and takes a lot of time to resolve. Law enforcement agencies are not prepared to prevent or resolve identity theft cases. It is up to each individual to protect personal information and to be aware of the possibility of identity theft.

As soon as police officers learn of an armed robbery or burglary in progress on the radio, their adrenaline starts pumping and they speed to the location, willing to put their lives in peril trying to catch a dangerous criminal. This zeal to respond is commendable and every year saves countless people from harm. The penalties for violent crimes are severe. If you are held up at gunpoint and deprived of a twenty-dollar bill, the perpetrator could serve ten years in a state prison.

The plus side of opportunistic thefts is that such crimes are over in an instant. A bank robber rarely takes more than two minutes to complete his mission; burglars like to strike with no one around and escape in the cover of darkness.

Unfortunately, the crime of the century is turning out to be one in which almost all the perpetrators get away scot-free after stealing identities, robbing their victims of tens of thousands of dollars (in some cases, hundreds of thousands of dollars), and devastating their lives for years. There is no emergency response to catch these criminals! Police and the criminal justice system until recently have shown little enthusiasm for tracking this crime and going after the perpetrators. Identity theft has turned into an extremely lucrative crime, and its impact on victims is horrendous. Victims are given the runaround by credit agencies, banks, mortgage companies, and businesses; police do not seem to be very helpful. Collection agencies hound victims to collect for purchases that were not made; as a result of their bad credit records, their loan applications are denied, they cannot rent apartments, and they cannot get jobs.

In commonly encountered crimes, the victim makes a police report and detectives conduct their investigation to find the perpetrator. Once the criminal is found, district attorneys file charges, the case goes to trial, and the judge metes out punishment. Unfortunately, in the case of identity theft, the victim is treated like a criminal by most agents in the criminal justice system for months, until the victim can prove that he is the victim of a crime. The average victim spends 175 hours and $808 in out-of-pocket expenses in clearing his name. Welcome to the twenty-first century and the crime of modern times.

What Is Identity Theft?

Identity theft occurs when someone steals your name and important information about you, including your Social Security number, credit card numbers, or your passwords and personal identification numbers (PIN) to make ATM withdrawals, shop on the Internet, gain access to your bank accounts, obtain loans and credit cards under your name, make unauthorized purchases, and open utility accounts. Often the criminal has run up forty to fifty thousand dollars in purchases before the victim even finds out that his identity has been stolen. Most people find out that they have been victims of identity theft months later, after their credit history has been destroyed.

Identity theft has skyrocketed in the last few years. According to recent FBI [Federal Bureau of Investigation] statistics, identity theft is the fastest growing white-collar crime in the United States. An estimated 500,000 to 750,000 Americans were victims of identity theft in 2001, which cost over $3 billion. These numbers don't reveal the true severity of the crime, as identity theft is vastly underreported. Identity theft has the potential to cause enormous damage to individuals as well as the national economy, eclipsing the effects of conventional crimes. No one is immune from this crime.

Although identity theft can wipe out someone's credit record for years, that is not the only way a victim suffers. Harrowing examples abound. For more than twelve years, a Florida suspect assumed and lived under the identity of a California victim, who had lost his wallet containing his driver's license and other personal information while vacationing in Daytona Beach in 1987. During that time, the suspect purchased and sold homes, opened bank accounts, obtained credit, established utility and phone service, and was arrested on at least three separate occasions. Based on a Florida warrant, the victim was wrongly arrested in California and held in jail for more than a week. Also, he faced civil judgments levied against him.

According to Secret Service testimony at a May 2001 congressional hearing, an investigation conducted jointly by the Secret Service and the New York Police Department revealed that the credit card accounts of many of the nation's wealthiest executives, as well as many other citizens, had been compromised. Using the Internet and cellular telephones, perpetrators obtained credit card account numbers, established fictitious addresses, and attempted to transfer approximately $22 million from the victims' legitimate brokerage and bank accounts into fraudulently established accounts for their own use. In October 2002, a 32-year-old restaurant worker pleaded guilty to breaching bank, brokerage, and credit card accounts belonging to the richest Americans, including billionaire Warren Buffet, in his scheme to steal over $80 million.

Law enforcement resources are totally inadequate to investigate identity theft.

Identity theft is not restricted to financial crimes alone. Illegal immigrants use identity theft to get false documents so they can work and also obtain permanent residency status. Federal investigations have shown that some aliens use fraudulent documents in connection with more serious illegal activities such as narcotics trafficking and potential terrorism. This is a cause for great concern. Terrorists can easily assume a legitimate identity and obtain driver's licenses and credit cards by stealing Social Security numbers of dead people. A U.S. Sentencing Commission report noted that "[a] World Trade Center defendant used, and was in possession of, numerous false identification documents, such as photographs, bank documents, medical histories, and education records from which numerous false identities could have been created." At a February 2002 congressional hearing, an FBI representative testified that various FBI field offices had begun to investigate fraud schemes having a potential to finance terrorists.

Why Is Identity Theft Increasing?

It is very easy for criminals to steal identities. Many credit grantors, for example, do not carefully check the identities of applicants before approving credit. One can be approved for credit cards and loans almost immediately without supplying much information. Coupled with this is the fact that identity theft has not yet received sufficient attention from law enforcement. Criminals have discovered that law enforcement resources are totally inadequate to investigate identity theft. They are rarely apprehended, let alone tried. In the rare cases when identity thieves are caught and tried, penalties are minimal and sadly seldom involve prison time; generally, the thieves are placed on probation or sentenced to community service. Why wouldn't criminals indulge in a highly profitable, nefarious enterprise if there is such a low probability of getting caught and punished?

The Los Angeles Police Department (LAPD) has been swamped by reports of identity theft. Each month, one bureau alone receives over three hundred reports of identity theft. As very few detectives are assigned to this crime, the workload is overwhelming. The LAPD is lucky to have financial crimes detectives, as most agencies do not have specialized units for identity theft. Due to complexities of the cases and noncooperation of creditors (most companies do not share data with police investigators and, instead of taking action, simply close accounts), the clearance rate for identity theft is even less than homicides—less than 2 percent of such cases end up being solved.

Police around the country have not been able to crack down on this crime for several reasons. First of all, identity theft is a "nontraditional" crime. Some police departments don't recognize the importance of taking reports of identity theft, much less initiating investigations. Furthermore, community and political pressures encourage police to allocate major resources toward violent crimes and drug offenses; thus, resources for addressing identity theft often are insufficient. Complicating the issue is the complex nature of the investigations required for identity theft. Many cases are multi- or cross-jurisdictional. A perpetrator may steal personal information in one city and use the information to conduct fraudulent activities in another city or state. Many law enforcement agencies tend to view identity theft as being "someone else's problem." The police in the victim's area of residence refer him to the police department in the county or state where the perpetrator used the information, but that police department may refer the victim back to the area-of-residence police department.

How Are Identities Stolen?

Technology has simplified most scams. Anyone with a computer, printer, and scanner can falsify personal checks, credit cards, and various forms of identification. Fake ID templates are available on the Internet. Every day, one million credit card offers are mailed to consumers; each minute, tens of thousands of credit card purchases are processed. Americans can open accounts, deposit money, and spend funds without speaking to a single person. Data that can be entered into a computer or on a telephone keypad are used to identify most customers.

It is amazing that stealing someone's identity requires so little effort. I can go online and find out names and mailing addresses of almost anyone by paying fifteen dollars. For a fee of sixty-five dollars, I can purchase Social Security numbers and employment information on the Internet—all in a matter of a few seconds! The privacy that we took for granted for years has suddenly become endangered due to the prevalence of high-speed computers and decryption software.

The first and foremost reason that identity theft has become rampant these days is the ease with which one can find out Social Security numbers. Social Security numbers are used as identification and account numbers by many entities, in fact, some states put Social Security numbers on their drivers' licenses. Insurance companies, universities, utility companies, banks, brokerages, and even department stores often have records of Social Security numbers, resulting in a glut of places where our Social Security numbers are floating around;

any thief can fish for them in this gold mine and use them to start new credit card accounts or apply for loans. In worst-case scenarios, someone may commit a crime in your name and have the law enforcement searching for you.

Thieves can obtain your Social Security number by stealing mail or sifting through the trash outside your residence. Workers at realties, banks, small businesses, and auto dealerships have easy access to them. Once a criminal gets your Social Security number, then the rest is easy.

Identities Are Stolen in Many Different Ways

Thieves have other strategies that require scant effort on their part. Think about the last time you opened your mailbox. How many unsolicited offers of preapproved credit cards did you find? The credit industry, in its zeal for profit, has made it too easy for people to get credit. In fact credit issuers mailed over 3 billion preapproved offers of credit to consumers last year; a typical household receives several solicitations per week. Many of these preapproved offers find their way into the hands of prowling identity-theft sharks.

Nonhuman customer support via touch-tone telephone and computer requires us to have many passwords (in technical speak, digital identification keys) to access services, especially paying bills or making purchases online. The advantages are that customers can do business twenty-four hours a day and companies save money. Unfortunately, besides the obvious social cost of removing human-to-human interaction, the potential damage is enormous. The proliferation of identification keys has created an environment that is conducive to identity theft. It is much easier to find someone's identification keys than to mug him. With the right keys to authenticate himself to a computer system as someone else, the criminal becomes that person. An identity thief can withdraw money from your account, transfer your assets from a stock portfolio, and even sell your house without your knowledge.

A more old-fashioned means of identity theft is to steal a purse or wallet. A few years ago, thieves were interested only in the cash inside your wallet; now the most valuable items in your wallet are your Social Security number, ATM card, credit cards, bank checks, and any other items containing your personal information.

The end result of stealing your identity is that a criminal takes advantage of your good name and leaves behind a bad one.

Identity thieves may get your personal information by posing over the phone, to be your employer, loan officer, or landlord and saying they need to get your credit report. Unfortunately there are few safeguards for consumer protection in the credit reporting business. Identity thieves may hang around banks and watch transactions at automated teller machines to capture your PIN. Criminals working in restaurants can download information from your credit card in seconds by swiping them in portable decoders or just simply copying down the numbers from the credit slip.

Increasing use of public records posted on the Internet by courts and public agencies has also helped identity thieves. The *New York Times* reported that a business manager in Cincinnati who used the Hamilton County Court's Web site to check on records of potential employees learned that easy access to public records can also hurt innocent people. Someone used the same site to steal this individual's personal details from a traffic citation he had received in 1996 and opened seven credit cards in his name, charging $11,000.

For those searching for jobs using the Internet, placing their resume online can expose them to identity theft. Identity thieves are getting critical information from resumes, such as date of birth, driver's license, and Social Security numbers, with the least amount of effort.

The end result of stealing your identity is that a criminal takes advantage of your good name and leaves behind a bad one. . . .

It is impossible to ensure that one will never be a victim of identity theft. As we devise better protective tools, criminals will find better ways of beating them. Still, by using common-sense measures, you can reasonably guard against identity theft.

8

Identity Theft Is Not a Growing Problem

Brian Bergstein

Brian Bergstein is a national technology reporter for the Associated Press.

The reported number of identity theft cases is inaccurate because there is no clear definition of what identity theft involves. Many people report crimes as identity theft, although further questioning reveals the crime as a different kind of fraud. Misleading statistics cause people to worry needlessly about identity theft. Government actions to prevent identity theft can disrupt normal business transactions. Identity theft does occur to a relatively small percentage of people. It is not as widespread as it may seem to be.

If some of the numbers being cited about identity theft are to be believed, it's just a matter of time before some unseen cyberhustler steals your name, empties your bank account and wrecks your financial reputation. You can almost hear the maniacal laughter.

By some measures, one in five Americans has been hit. Another common statistic is that 10 million people fall victim every year. Making matters even scarier, new laws in California and other states have forced companies to essentially tell all U.S. consumers when their personal data have been com-

Brian Bergstein, "ID Theft Numbers May Be Misleading; The Problem of Identity Theft Can Be Too Broadly Defined and Is Often Misunderstood, Leading to Potential Inflation of the Numbers of People Involved and the Misdirection of Public Policy Debates," *InformationWeek*, November 15, 2005.

promised—even if the files have not actually been maliciously used. In response, Congress is considering bills to restrict the flow of personal information. And identity theft monitoring services have sprung up that can cost consumers well over $100 a year.

But while it's certainly important to be vigilant against this potentially devastating crime, it also appears identity theft is too broadly defined and often misunderstood. As a result, some experts say, lawmakers and companies might be misdirecting their anti-fraud energies. Overly fearful consumers could be unnecessarily avoiding doing business on the Web.

Too often overlooked, many analysts argue, are savvy "synthetic" fraud schemes that frequently don't directly victimize individual consumers. In such schemes, criminals invent fictitious identities and use them to ring up phony charges. By some estimates, this accounts for three-quarters of the money stolen by identity crooks.

"There's a lot of fraud that is not being identified as fraud, not being measured accurately," said Anne Wallace, executive director of the Identity Theft Assistance Center, an industry-funded group that helps victims resolve fraud problems for free. "It's written off as bad debt. It's bad debt because the guy didn't exist."

Understanding the Real Risk

To understand the risks we really face, it's worth analyzing the statistics. Multiple surveys have found that around 20 percent of Americans say they have been beset by identity theft. But what exactly is identity theft? The Identity Theft and Assumption Deterrence Act of 1998 defines it as the illegal use of someone's "means of identification"—including a credit card. So if you lose your card and someone else uses it to buy a candy bar, technically you have been the victim of identity theft.

Of course misuse of lost, stolen, or surreptitiously copied credit cards is a serious matter. But it shouldn't force anyone to hide in a cave. Federal law caps our personal liability at $50, and even that amount is often waived. That's why surveys have found that about two-thirds of people classified as identity theft victims end up paying nothing out of their own pockets.

The more pernicious versions of identity theft, in which fraudsters use someone else's name to open lines of credit or obtain government documents, are much rarer. Consider a February survey for insurer Chubb Corp. of 1,866 people nationwide. Nearly 21 percent said they had been an identity theft victim in the previous year. But when the questioners asked about specific circumstances—and broadened the time frame beyond just the previous year—the percentages diminished. About 12 percent said a collection agency had demanded payment for purchases they hadn't made. Some 8 percent said fraudulent checks had been drawn against their accounts.

In both cases, the survey didn't ask whether a faulty memory or a family member—rather than a shadowy criminal—turned out to be the culprit. It wouldn't be uncommon. In a 2005 study by Synovate, a research firm, half of victims who determined who was to blame pinned it on relatives, friends, neighbors, or in-home employees. When Chubb's report asked whether people had suffered the huge headache of finding that someone else had taken out loans in their name, 2.4 percent—one in 41 people—said yes.

So what about the claim that 10 million Americans are hit every year, a number often used to pitch credit monitoring services? That statistic, which would amount to about one in 22 adults, also might not be what it seems.

The figure arose in a 2003 report by Synovate commissioned by the Federal Trade Commission [FTC]. A 2005 update by Synovate put the figure closer to 9 million. Both totals include misuse of existing credit cards. Subtracting that, the identity theft numbers were still high but not as frightful: The FTC report determined that fraudsters had opened new accounts or committed similar misdeeds in the names of 3.2 million Americans in the previous year. The average victim lost $1,180 and wasted 60 hours trying to resolve the problem. Clearly, it's no picnic.

Oversimplifying identity theft has big consequences . . . it confuses people trying to determine their level of risk.

But there was one intriguing nugget deep in the report. Some 38 percent of identity theft victims said they hadn't bothered to notify anyone—not the police, not their credit card company, not a credit bureau. Even when fraud losses purportedly exceeded $5,000, the kept-it-to-myself rate was 19 percent. Perhaps some people decide that raising a stink over a wrongful charge isn't worth the trouble. Even so, the finding made the overall validity of the data seem questionable to Fred Cate, an Indiana University law professor who specializes in privacy and security issues.

"That's not identity theft," he said. "I'm just confident if you saw a charge that wasn't yours, you'd contact somebody."

Inaccurate Statistics Cause Problems

Now, you might say, who cares if statistics are inflated or misleading? After all, identity theft remains widespread even by conservative measurements. And companies that handle our personal information still could go to greater lengths to protect it—often simply by encrypting their files.

To Julia Cheney, an industry specialist at the Payment Cards Center in the Federal Reserve Bank of Philadelphia, oversimplifying identity theft has big consequences. For one thing, she believes it confuses people trying to determine their level of risk. That could lead many consumers to unnecessarily shy away from Internet commerce, or drive them into the arms of costly protection vendors instead of making regular scans of their credit reports—a process that is now free. Cheney also believes the muddled definitions make it harder for financial firms to assess their countermeasures and trickier for law enforcement to monitor trends.

It also could throw lawmakers off course as they consider solutions. For example, several identity theft measures pending in Congress are focused on curtailing the use and transfer of personal data. But companies that scan for the manipulations employed by "synthetic" fraudsters have said some proposals—such as restrictions on the dissemination of Social Security numbers—actually might inhibit their work.

The bills also don't appear to address loopholes in the credit system that let synthetic fraud flourish. "It may be a big problem, but it's not the big problem that policymakers and legislators are talking about right now," Cate said. "We're tilting at the wrong windmill."

9

Internet Pornography Harms Society

Richard Jerome

Richard Jerome is a writer for People *magazine.*

Internet pornography is readily available to teenagers and younger children. Viewing pornographic images distorts a young person's understanding of sex, intimacy, relationships, and respect for themselves and each other. Young people can become addicted to Internet porn, and are often exposed to extreme sexual behaviors that are far outside social norms. Although it is too early to determine the long-term effects that Internet pornography will have on young people, some young people already struggle to maintain healthy relationships with members of the opposite sex.

At suburban Riverdale Public School in New Jersey, a visitor recently posed a question to an eighth-grade class: "Have you seen Internet pornography?" All 42 students raised their hands.

One of them was 13-year-old Ryan Cleary, who admits to looking at Internet porn occasionally as a kind of research tool, so he'll know more about what he's supposed to do with girlfriends. "Guys will ask if I've gone to first base yet, so I got to figure things out. If you don't know, they laugh at you," he says. "Some guys look at porn out of curiosity and to figure out what they want to do with girls in the future."

Richard Jerome, "The Cyberporn Generation: As the First Kids to Grow Up with Internet Porn Come of Age, Researchers Look at How Online Porn Can Color a Child's View of Love and Sex," *People*, vol. 61.16, April 26, 2004, p. 72.

Like all teens, Ryan's classmate Stephanie Struniewski, also 13, is blasted with beauty images everywhere from magazines to MTV. Yet she blames her ex-boyfriend's interest in Internet porn for playing havoc with her self-image. "He told me he wanted me to look skinny like the porn girls," she says. "He told me I was fat, that I was a hippo."

The Cyberporn Generation

Meet the cyberporn generation. According to a study by the Henry J. Kaiser Family Foundation, 70 percent of the nation's 15- to 17-year-olds have looked at Internet pornography, much of it graphically hardcore. The notion of adolescents peeping at risque images is hardly novel, of course. And the Web, with its 24-hour anonymity and infinite variety—an estimated 1 million erotic Web sites, with chat rooms, video feeds and cascading porn pop-ups—superseded that tattered *Playboy* stashed under little Biff's mattress years ago.

But now the first generation of kids who have never known a world without Internet porn is coming of age at a time when the culture at large is grappling with shifting standards of what constitutes decent exposure. "In the past, we had boundaries," says psychologist Mary Ann Layden, director of education at the University of Pennsylvania's Center for Cognitive Therapy. "Now Paris Hilton, Pam [Pamela Anderson] and Tommy Lee make videos of themselves having sex. So the message is that it's normal to watch people having sex."

Nowhere is this new normal more evident, influential or accessible than on the Net. "The Internet provides a cookbook to kids and will become the de facto sex educator, not the parents, not the schools," says behavioral scientist Ralph DiClemente of Atlanta's Emory University, who has launched a $3 million, five-year study of kids and cyberporn sponsored by the National Institute of Mental Health. Research is in its infancy, but experts on teen behavior say they're starting to see troubling results suggesting Internet porn could be distorting kids' views about sex.

"Younger kids may not have much world experience, and Internet porn could shape their norms about relationships," DiClemente says. With high-speed downloading, he adds, the difference between *Playboy* and Web porn is like that between riding a burro versus taking a Concorde. "Kids may wonder if it's okay to degrade their partner. They may dissociate sex from intimacy. Trying to bring those two elements together down the road may be very difficult."

Lasting Effects

For some more than others. Troy Busher was 12 the first time he saw pornography on the Internet—and he looked at it almost every day for the next nine years. "It's all about female submission: 'You're my ho. Get down on your knees,'" he says. When he finally got a real girlfriend in high school, "she pretty much became like garbage to me," says Busher, now 25 and a college student in Fullerton, Calif. "I was always demanding more, putting my hands in the wrong places. I acted like her body was mine and I could do what I wanted." For those who are easily influenced by such images, it's hard not to return to them, says psychiatrist Dr. Richard Blankenship, owner and director of the North Atlanta Center for Professional Counseling and Psychiatry. Graphic porn images, he says, make the brain "light up like a Christmas tree." Which explains why Busher says, "I have more memories of porn than of childhood."

Of course, pornographers argue that—in the right hands—porn has its place. As anyone in the industry will readily proclaim, millions of men and women enjoy Web erotica harmlessly, and some couples turn to porn to enhance their sex lives. Insiders also stress that the vast majority of adult sites are precisely that and have no interest in attracting children.

"I'm happy to say most people who contact us do ask about how to keep out kids," says Kevin Godbee, director of sales for a Boca Raton, Fla., company that operates as an "adult chamber of commerce" and publishes an Internet-porn trade magazine. "It's a very, very small percentage of people involved in this industry that don't have the highest moral and ethical standards."

If kids have a problem, many parents don't know.

But there's no question that hard-core sexual and violent images are readily available to kids on the Net. "I swear I receive 200 porn e-mails a day," says Riverdale student Nick Homcy, 14. "I've not only seen a man and a woman having sex on the Internet, but a man, a woman and a donkey." According to the Kaiser study, 83 percent of 15- to 17-year-olds have Internet access at home—a third of them in their bedrooms. It used to be that "when a 15-year-old looked at *Playboy*, he had to put it away quickly because his dad was coming," says psychologist Layden. "Now kids can end up at torture sites."

Even if kids aren't looking for porn, it will find them, through links in spam e-mails, instant messages and recurring pop-up ads, a practice known as mousetrapping that can sometimes only be stopped by going to a site or shutting down the computer. Filters only do so much. "Any kid with any kind of smarts can get around a filter," says Jason, 20, a college student who only recently swore off Internet porn. Besides, he adds, "I would go to 20 sites, and 18 would be filtered—there were always two or so that wouldn't be."

The Need for Parental Supervision

If that comes as a surprise to parents, Herbert Lin of the National Research Council has two words: Pay attention. At the behest of Congress, Lin led a 2002 project on Youth, Pornography and the Internet. What he learned was "how clueless parents are about what their kids do on the Internet," he says. "If kids have a problem, many parents don't know."

Debbie Holt's two teenage boys didn't have a problem, and she always gave them privacy and space. Then the Maryland insurance broker received a suspicious bill from a place called Alyon Technologies, charging $184 for "adult content." It turned out that her 14-year-old had clicked on a pop-up window that led him to a porn site. "I'm not such a strict parent that I ban my kids from seeing R-rated movies," she says. "But what bothered me about this was that I had absolutely no idea what they were seeing. They could have seen two kids going at it."

Above all, Holt was incensed that it had all happened so easily: When a proof-of-age box appeared, her son clicked "Yes, I am 18," and the site began billing by the minute. So she lodged complaints with congressmen, police and the Federal Trade Commission [FTC]. The Maryland attorney general's office and the FTC pressured Alyon, which finally refunded her money eight months later. (She also started a Web site for other concerned parents but shut it down after it was overrun with postings by pornographers.) "If kids want to buy cigarettes, the [vendor] has to card them," she says, adding that online purchases usually require some personal info, such as a credit card number. "What child is going to say, 'Uh-uh, my parents said I couldn't go into that site'?"

As the father of an 8-year-old boy, James DiGiorgio understands that frustration. But as a producer of porn movies, about 90 percent of which wind up on the Internet, he grows somewhat defensive. Though Jimmy D., as he is known, admits that some in the industry are unscrupulous about luring children, "I don't think we're the only business that is sometimes promoting an unhealthy view of the world and sexuality," he says. DiGiorgio believes it's a parent's responsibility to protect kids from seeing porn on the Net. "My son is not going to get on the Internet without supervision from me or my wife. Parents need to be very, very involved."

But even the most involved parent can feel helpless in the face of irrepressibly curious teens. Craig Nelson, a financial consultant in Orange County, Calif., has two teenage sons and a computer. Do the math. "I went into the computer history one day, and sure enough, there were a few pornography Web sites," says Nelson, 49. "I figured they had stumbled onto it." When those sites kept proliferating in the history, Nelson confronted the boys and moved their desktop to the family room. When the PC gave out, he bought a wireless laptop. Unable to trust the boys alone at home with it, he began taking the computer along whenever he and his wife went out to dinner. In the house, he made the boys sit at the kitchen bar, in plain sight, when going online.

It seemed like a good idea at the time. But "they'll visit 25, 30, 40 different [porn] sites with their mom standing there cooking," says Nelson, awed by their brazenness. "A couple of nights ago, I was walking upstairs and back down again and in that two or three minutes my older son looked at some porn and then got out of it." Nelson has since installed a password known only to him and his wife, so their sons can go online only when a parent is present. When he discusses his dilemma with other parents, he's stunned by their denials. "I ask if their kids struggle with pornography on the Internet, and 99.9 percent say, 'No, not at all,'" Nelson says. "I have no doubt that they're being naive."

10

Internet Pornography Benefits Society

Annalee Newitz

Annalee Newitz is a contributing editor for Wired *and former policy analyst at the Electronic Frontier Foundation. She writes a weekly syndicated column called Techsploitation and has contributed to* New Scientist, *the* New York Times, *the* Wall Street Journal, Popular Science, *and* AlterNet. *Newitz received a Knight Science Journalism Fellowship in 2002 and was a research fellow at the Massachusetts Institute of Technology (MIT).*

The pornography industry leads the development of new technologies to promote online privacy and freedom of speech. Innovative software that ensures anonymous Web surfing was initially created to help distribute Internet pornography, but also helps political activists and human rights workers. Technological advancements made by the pornography industry protect civil liberties for all Internet users.

The makers of [video game] *Grand Theft Auto: San Andreas* [GTA] are facing an investigation by the US Federal Trade Commission after it emerged that explicit sex scenes were hidden inside the popular game's software.

The discovery provoked a wave of condemnation from politicians, including an accusation by Republican congressman Fred Upton that GTA's publisher, Take-Two, had "bla-

Annalee Newitz, "Why We All Need Pornography: Porn Fans Are the Driving Force Behind Technologies That We Might One Day All Rely On to Protect Our Identity," *New Scientist*, vol. 2511, August 6, 2005, p. 24.

tantly circumvented the rules in order to peddle sexually explicit material to our youth".

But it is not the first time technology has been used to offer people a sneaky peek at sex. The "adult entertainment" industry embraced video cassettes, DVDs and the Web more quickly than its mainstream counterparts because these media are tailor-made for private viewing. Consumers eager for a glimpse of skin, but afraid of being found out or of being spotted in a seedy blue-movie [adult-movie] cinema, helped drive the demand for more of these technologies.

In the process, they are making the internet a more hospitable place for those promoting racial, ethnic or religious hatred, or even organizing terrorist attacks. But it will also help political dissidents and whistle-blowers, so technologies created to help porn enthusiasts today are the human rights' tools of tomorrow.

Better Privacy Online

Nick Mathewson, a Boston-based software developer working on a cutting-edge internet anonymity network called Tor, says privacy is not just a porn problem. "It's for issues like health information and political speech. We're trying to offer privacy and anonymity to everyone—we don't distinguish what we feel that people should and shouldn't have access to."

Like many new tools that promise privacy online, Tor is a response to the fact that the Internet does not guarantee anonymity any more. Website software often creates logs full of information about who you are and what you click on, even after you've left the site. And new analytical techniques make it easier for eavesdroppers to figure out where you're going online, and where you're coming from.

That's why the next decade may usher in a progression from the physical privacy of the Web, which hides what you're doing from your next-door neighbours, to systems such as Tor that give you online anonymity, hiding what you're doing from snoopers on computer networks.

More Freedom of Speech

But publishers of online porn aren't just facing new technological challenges—there are legal ones too. Several high-profile Internet obscenity cases are working their way through the US courts. Barbara Nitke, the plaintiff in one of them, is a New York-based photographer of adult images who has challenged the definition of obscenity in US law. The Communications Decency Act says it is illegal to transmit content via the Internet that "appeals to the prurient interest" and is deemed offensive by "contemporary community standards".

Nitke argues that this law restricts free speech. Because her website of explicit photographs can be viewed by anyone in the US, she feels there is a constant threat that some community might deem it offensive by their local standards and charge her with obscenity. Her suit challenges the idea that "community standards" that follow real-world borders can be applied to the internet, as it is a global entity.

When Nitke's case was heard in a New York court last year [in 2004], the US government argued that community standards could be maintained online through the use of geolocation software. Most such software works by checking the unique internet protocol (IP) address on a website visitor's computer, and matching it to a geographical place using a variety of methods, such as the registered location of the visitor's Internet service provider (ISP).

The court announced on 25 July [2005] that it had failed to make a decision on the use of geolocation software to maintain community standards, and the case is now on appeal to a higher court.

Ubiquitous geolocation on the Internet would kill the idea of anonymity online. "Geolocation would destroy people's sense of privacy and freedom," says Nitke. "As soon as you know your personal proclivities are open for the government to know about, it's a huge wet blanket."

But Ben Laurie, a London-based computer security expert with A. L. Digital, is sceptical that geolocation could be effective on any broad scale. "None of this software works," he says. "Geolocation by IP address is all you've got, and that's determined by where cables run and where your ISP is, which has bugger all to do with legal jurisdictions." In other words, an IP address might tell you where somebody's ISP is, but that might be hundreds of kilometres or more from where he or she lives. It certainly won't reveal what community standard should be applied to the person in question. Nevertheless, if Nitke's case reaches the US Supreme Court, it is possible the judges will rule that geolocation software be used to enforce geographical community standards online.

Anonymous Web Surfing

But if history is any indication, efforts to track people's whereabouts as they peruse porn are doomed to fail. The urge to remain unseen has already driven many to use anonymous proxies—computers that substitute their own IP addresses for yours to shield your true location. It's not just for the tech-savvy: Anonymizer in San Diego, California, offers an anonymous surfing package that routes all your Web activities through an anonymous proxy to mask your IP address.

Whether a conversation is about naughty fantasies or human rights' violations, spies won't be able to find out who was talking or what was said.

More sophisticated solutions, such as Tor, don't just hide your personal IP address but also mask your location from snoops who try to hunt you down with a technique called "traffic analysis", which works out the pathway your communications take over the Internet. When you're surfing the Web, or sending and receiving emails, Tor routes your data through its network of servers, which encrypt your communication while also creating arbitrary and constantly changing paths for it through the Tor network. As a result, your IP address will appear different every time you visit a given website. And it's extremely difficult for somebody to find out where your messages are coming from by following them back through the Tor network.

"I would definitely expect people to use a tool like Tor to get around geolocation," says Roger Dingledine, who works with Mathewson on Tor development. "Part of the goal of Tor is to put all the users on neutral ground, so they can't be singled out and treated differently based on where they're coming from." Tor has received funding from the US navy, which is interested in using the technology to snoop at websites without being identified, as well as San Francisco-based civil liberties group the Electronic Frontier Foundation.

Other researchers, such as Ian Goldberg, the chief scientist of security specialist Zero-Knowledge Systems, are developing ways to exchange instant messages while shielding users from being identified. Goldberg's Off-the-Record (OTR) messaging protocol allows people to send messages using encryption keys that are discarded after each use, so even if a snooper finds the key for one messaging session, they cannot decrypt another session. Whether the conversation is about naughty fantasies or human rights' violations, spies won't be able to find out who was talking or what was said.

Now that technical developments and social forces have left the Web about as private as a room of surveillance cameras, it is often the secretive hunt for porn that creates a market for new technologies such as Tor and OTR messaging. In turn we end up with tools that can also be used to promote liberty and justice. That's good news for political dissidents and human rights workers—as well as anyone who feels their browsing is nobody's business but their own.

11

Social-Networking Sites Contribute to Crime

Bill Hewitt

Bill Hewitt is a writer, journalist, and contributor to numerous magazines and Web sites.

Social-networking sites such as MySpace are popular with teenagers. However, these sites can prove to be dangerous for young people who give out too much personal information, engage in conversations with strangers, or develop friendships with strangers who may not be representing themselves truthfully. Social-networking sites have been shown to attract sexual predators looking to take advantage of naïve young people. Parents should be involved and have some knowledge of what their children are doing online, especially in relation to social-networking sites.

When it comes to using MySpace, the explosively popular Web site for kids and young adults, Niki Martin and her 12-year-old daughter Ashley have a deal. "She only talks to her friends from school," says Niki. But on Feb. 26 [2006] Ashley happened to be visiting a neighbor in Vancouver, Wash., when she logged onto her MySpace page, which was decorated with pictures of herself playing softball, and noticed an e-mail from a stranger that said, "Hey, beautiful, we should get together sometime."

What unfolded next was a chilling object lesson in how children are now closer than ever to the dark alleys of the Web. Alerted by Ashley to the message, the neighbor, 26-year-

Bill Hewitt, "MySpace Nation: The Controversy," *People*, vol. 65.22, June 5, 2006, p. 113.

old Adrienne Sylvester, slid in front of the keyboard and pretended to be the 12-year-old. Within minutes the man was asking what kind of underwear the girl had on and soon afterward was streaming video to her MySpace page of himself performing a sexual act—footage that Sylvester had the presence of mind to capture on a camcorder pointed at the monitor. Sylvester, who meanwhile had summoned police, made arrangements to meet the man nearby. An hour later when Jeramie Ray Eidem, 26, pulled into the parking lot of a fast-food restaurant, he was arrested. (He is now being held on charges of attempted rape of a child, to which he has pleaded not guilty.) And while he never laid a finger on Ashley, that does not mean she was untouched by the episode. "She knew what was going on," says her mother, Niki, "and she was shocked."

MySpace Controversy

And she is not alone. Launched two years ago [in 2004], MySpace has swiftly become one of the biggest hits in the history of the Internet. A social networking site meant to share music, foster new friendships and a sense of community, it now boasts 80 million members and is second only to Yahoo in the number of page views per day—making it by far the biggest player in the Web's networking niche, which also includes such sites as Facebook and Xanga. Geared for teens and young adults—20 percent of the site's visitors are between 14 and 17—MySpace owes much of its popularity to the fact that, unlike old-fashioned chat rooms, it allows members to upload photographs and video clips to their own pages and include information about themselves. But along with success MySpace has also generated considerable controversy. Crimes as serious as murder and rape have been linked to teens using the site, which has also become a preferred venue for cyberbullies and online pedophiles. Kids have posted tales—and photos—of their alleged drinking and drug use. Even a casual visitor can quickly encounter raunchy, explicit sexual advice or memoirs. As a result, a growing number of schools around the country have blocked access to the site. "Everywhere I go, parents and teachers are very concerned about MySpace," says Dr. David Walsh, a psychologist who heads the Minneapolis-based National Institute on Media and the Family. "In the past two months it's been on everyone's radar."

MySpace cofounder Chris DeWolfe insists the company takes its responsibility for preventing misuse of the site very seriously. He points out that nearly a third of its 300 employees are assigned to review content and take down anything objectionable, and that the company offers a 24-hour hotline to work with law enforcement on catching online predators. "Much of what we do revolves around user policing and deputizing users to report abuse," says DeWolfe, 40. "From a policing standpoint we put a lot of effort into this site." On April 10 [2006] the company announced that it had hired a former federal prosecutor to oversee security on the site.

People will write and say, "You're hot. Let's hang out." And it turns out the person who wrote it is some 40-year-old guy with kids.

There is no denying the enormous power and appeal of MySpace among teens. It is not uncommon for kids to log on repeatedly to their pages to check for new postings from friends. C.J. Freeman, 16, of LaOtto, Ind., admits that she goes three times a day to her page, which contains photos, snippets from her favorite music, comments from her boyfriend and bits of trivia about herself (she's lactose intolerant, loves sports, hates health food). "It's a great way to keep in touch and to meet new friends," she says. "You can really personalize your space." Says psychologist Walsh: "Kids have always congregated with other kids. Two generations ago, it was at the corner candy store. Now, in this high-tech age, MySpace is the candy store on steroids."

Freeman's mother, Teresa, takes some basic precautions. For example, she insists that the computer be in the family room so that she can keep tabs on her daughter's computer activity. But ultimately, she trusts her daughter's judgment. "There are probably some things on the site that would make me uncomfortable," she says. "But if I sat in the backseat of her car on one of her dates I would probably be uncomfortable too."

The Dangers Are Real

Parents who visit the site can come away shaken all the same. "It's totally blowing their minds," says John Shehan, manager of the CyberTipline of the National Center for Missing and Exploited Children. "They think of the diaries they kept when they were younger and can't imagine anyone reading what they've written—and it's the same stuff their kids are putting out there." Shellee Davies, 42, of Centerville, Utah, who has two daughters, Lindsay, 17, and Whitney, 14, who have been using the site for about six months, concluded that even more innocuous material could pose a threat. Prompted by a local news report about MySpace, she decided to have a look at her kids' sites for herself. "Until then," she says, "I was just clueless." What she found disturbed her, including entries on her daughters' MySpace pages that mentioned the schools they attended and their birthdays. She told the girls to delete anything that could make them targets—which Lindsay and Whitney were almost relieved to do. "It was okay with me because it can sometimes be kind of creepy," says Lindsay. "People will write and say, 'You're hot. Let's hang out.' And it turns out the person who wrote it is some 40-year-old guy with kids."

With younger kids, the risks are even greater. MySpace is supposedly restricted to users 14 and over. But there is nothing to prevent a younger child with an e-mail address from lying about his or her age and signing up as a member. And when they, as well as anyone else, venture on the site they can quickly be exposed to raw content. In New Hampshire, Det. James McLaughlin of the Keene Police Dept., who specializes in catching Internet predators, is astonished by some of what he stumbles upon. "Some kids perform sexual acts on Web cams," he says. "We'd like to think it's from socially isolated kids, but some of them are high-achieving kids who are sound socially. Parents can't believe it." Det. Ali Bartley, 30, of the Boulder County [Colorado] Sheriff's office got her first taste of MySpace in February, when she began investigating an alleged rape of an 18-year-old woman who said she met her attacker through a mutual friend on the site. "I'm not a prude," says Bartley. "But I was shocked when I started looking through MySpace."

When you grow up the first thing your parents teach you is to look both ways before you cross the street and to not get in cars with strangers. It's very similar for the Internet.

Yet pornography may not be the most troubling issue. As with any place popular with kids in the brick-and-mortar world, MySpace attracts more than its share of pedophiles, who comb through entries looking for clues to vulnerability. Scarcely a week goes by without news of a predator nabbed on MySpace. In March five teenage boys in Fontana, Calif., went on MySpace and created a profile of a 15-year-old girl as a prank. Instead they drew the attention of a 48-year-old man who agreed to meet the "girl" in a local park. The boys went to the park and when the man showed up summoned police, who arrested the suspect. While praising the kids, police caution against civilians using such ruses. "This isn't something

I'd suggest that other people try to reel in sexual predators," says Sgt. William Megenney of the Fontana police. "This could have turned ugly real quick."

Parents Should Be Involved

Not surprisingly some experts have concluded that parents should simply discourage kids from going on MySpace at all. "Get off of it," says Det. Dan Jackman of the Louisville, Ky., police's Crimes Against Children Unit. "There's no way to tell who is a pedophile and who is not." But that is far from a unanimous opinion. Debbie Beach, a therapist in northern Virginia who specializes in treating adolescents, points out that MySpace can offer some distinct benefits to teens. "MySpace and other sites open up a world where they can test out who they are and who they want to be," maintains Beach. "They can write uncensored, they can test out identities anonymously."

As for Niki Martin, she stifled her impulse to pull Ashley off the Web altogether. "That would have been like I was punishing her for doing the right thing," says Niki. Instead Ashley's Internet time is down to 15 minutes a day. To MySpace co-founder DeWolfe, that sort of measured response makes perfect sense. "The problems of the offline world are the same problems of the online world," he says. "When you grow up the first thing your parents teach you is to look both ways before you cross the street and to not get in cars with strangers. It's very similar for the Internet."

12

Social-Networking Sites Do Not Contribute to Crime

Gary Stager

Gary Stager is editor at-large for District Administration *magazine and an adjunct professor at Pepperdine University in California. In addition to writing a monthly column about education, he lectures and leads workshops at national conferences.*

Social-networking sites serve many positive and useful purposes for young people. There are risks in any activity that brings young people in contact with strangers, and social-networking sites are no more dangerous than any other pastime. Social-networking sites include numerous security measures to protect young users. The occurrence of crime that is directly related to these sites is low. Adults are being overly protective of young people with regard to use of social-networking sites.

During seventh grade a friend and I created a publication as an alternative to the school newspaper. It was quite a challenge in the days before access to photocopiers, but entertaining our handful of readers made the effort worthwhile.

I remember the day when the faculty advisor of the official school newspaper followed me into the boy's room, threw my 50-pound body against the wall and threatened to kill me if we published another issue. The English faculty's Tony Soprano [tough guy] really schooled me in the subtleties of the First Amendment. Ah, life was so much simpler then.

Gary Stager, "Guess Why They Call It MySpace? It's Time for Adults to Grow Up," *District Administration*, vol. 42.5, May 2006, pp. 78–79.

Since man first scribbled on cave walls and peed in the snow, humans have been compelled to share their stories. Recent decades have seen great violence done to student expression through court-sanctioned censorship of student publications and other forms of adult supremacy. Issues of critical importance and interest to students are banned from student newspapers and classroom discussions. Political correctness and tolerance are used to masquerade for intolerant policies like "zero-tolerance" and increasingly mediocre curriculum. High school credit is awarded just to get kids to contribute to some school newspapers.

Back in the good old days of lavatory justice, children climbed trees, played ball in the street and joined the scouts so they could play with fire. Santa delivered chemistry sets complete with recipes for gunpowder and kids could get together without having "my people call your people." You could actually read all 30 pages of *Sarah Plain and Tall* without a textbook publisher excerpting it for you. Remember when you could read a book without being interrupted every paragraph to answer a comprehension question?

Children Are Being Restricted Too Much

Parents and educators have done a lot more to wreck childhood than Tim Berners-Lee [the inventor of the World Wide Web] (ask a kid to show you how to learn about him at Wikipedia). Schools endanger the very students they seek to protect when they bubble-wrap kids and the curriculum. School principals are banning classic plays like *Grease* and *The Crucible* while childish schlock like *Seussical* is now the most performed high school musical. [Educator] John Taylor-Gatto argues that the mission of schools is now to extend childishness through graduation. Dependency and fear retard the learning process. It is difficult, if not impossible, for students to develop moral values and solve ethical dilemmas when school never allows them to make a decision or mistake.

Every generation has had to wrestle with understanding new media. In 1954, the U.S. Senate held hearings to investigate how comic books harm children. Who can forget Tipper Gore vs. Frank Zappa [1985 testimony at a congressional hearing about music censorship] or the 1995 *Time* magazine cover depicting a computer induced zombie child with CyberPorn in block letters? The educational technology community has a similar level of paranoia manifest in discussions over whether students should have their own floppy, be allowed to save on the hard drive, surf the Web, send an e-mail or use a USB key. It is impossible to discern the lines between genuine safety concerns and tyranny.

We should avoid destroying the place twenty-first century kids built for themselves.

The latest episode of adults behaving badly involves the hysteria over the popular Web site, MySpace. MySpace is a social networking site where anyone can publish and maintain relationships with friends. Chances are that your only experience with MySpace has come through local TV news stories about how parents must rescue their teenagers from this deadly cyber-sewer before sports and weather. It's a fair bet that you are not one of MySpace's 66 million registered users. There has probably never been a more aptly named product. They call it MySpace because it belongs to them, not you.

MySpace provides users with Web space where they may share their thoughts and creative output with classmates and friends around the world. What makes sites like MySpace different from other blogging sites is that you may ask interesting people to be your friend. Then you'll know when your friends are online, who their friends are and quickly develop affinity groups. You may organize communities around interests, geography or a host of other variables. You can chat via instant messages, insert music in your page and share all the photos and doodads that kids use to decorate their locker. (If school still trusts them with lockers.)

In fact, more than one observer has compared MySpace pages to a teenager's bedroom walls. My 12th grade daughter's MySpace site is unbearable. Animated gifs [graphic interchange formats], flashing graphics, dopey poses, horrific music, yellow text on hot pink backgrounds and other elements of Web design hell assault your senses until you run away or quit the browser. Much of MySpace's content is inane, but we should avoid destroying the place 21st century kids built for themselves.

As our government strives to spread democracy abroad, we would be well served by celebrating the electronic democracy afforded by sites like MySpace.

Evaluating the Risks

Sure there are creeps using MySpace. That's why you need to teach children not to share personal information online or get in a car with strangers. MySpace never shows the real name of a member, just a pseudonym like a CB radio handle. When you add a person to your friends list, that person receives an e-mail asking for permission. If someone turns out to be unpleasant, you may ban him or her from contacting you with a click. Even critics of MySpace concede the company is incredibly responsive to concerns over online ickyness. A student may be at greater risk of being suspended by her school for something written at home on MySpace as there is of that teenager being physically harmed.

MySpace is changing how young people communicate, collaborate and spend their discretionary funds. Network TV programs are being launched on MySpace and countless bands have experienced enormous sales due to word-of-mouth and users sharing music with their friends. The recent student walkouts over the proposed immigration bill were organized on MySpace. The role such sites play in grassroots and electoral politics is inestimable.

Today my daughter's high school experienced a small fire. She learned of the fire from friends via MySpace nearly 11 hours before the local television news reported it. MySpace is a teenager's record store, newsstand, community center, fan club and 24/7 news network. As our government strives to spread democracy abroad, we would be well served by celebrating the electronic democracy afforded by sites like MySpace.

I just learned that my daughter has retaliated for me showing her MySpace site in conference presentations by posting an unflattering photo of me online. I wonder if I can get the local school district to punish her?

13

Cyberbullying Is a Growing Problem

Rachel Simmons

Rachel Simmons authored Odd Girl Out: The Hidden Culture of Aggression in Girls, *and has appeared on various television and radio programs to speak about bullying and female aggression. She is a former Rhodes Scholar and is the founding director of the Girls Leadership Institute.*

Cyberbullying is becoming more prevalent among children of all ages. The Internet allows bullying to follow children into their homes, and it can occur at any time of the day or night. Young bullies are exploiting technology such as instant messaging and social-networking sites to torment their peers. Parents and schools are not doing enough to prevent cyberbullying.

The anonymous warning on the Internet bulletin board was posted to a popular eighth-grader at an exclusive Washington-area private school for girls. "I feel like throwing up just thinking of you," the author wrote, in a diatribe that soon degenerated into the frantic, grammarless prose so characteristic of children's online messaging. "Everything you do is just a ploy to raise your popularity. . . . u slut. . . . You may think ur safe now, but ur so gonna take a plunge down the popularity level, it is inevitable. . . . Most of us realize what a [expletive] loser you are, even if your few slaves don't."

The posted messages grew more menacing by the day, but it was not until the targeted girl was urged to kill herself that school officials were alerted and intervened, demanding that students delete their postings from the much-visited Web site.

Say hello to the newest strain of the bullying virus, technologically updated for the 21st century.

A recent spate of lawsuits against underage music pirates has finally focused adults' attention on teenage ethics and the Internet, but the news about what's been happening while grownups weren't looking is alarming. The Internet has transformed the landscape of children's social lives, moving cliques from lunchrooms and lockers to live chats and online bulletin boards, and intensifying their reach and power. When conflicts arise today, children use their expertise with interactive technologies to humiliate and bully their peers, and avoid reprimand from adults or foes. As parents plead technological ignorance with a my-Danny-hooks-everything-up sort of pride and many schools decline to discipline "off-campus" behavior, the Internet has become a free-for-all where bullying and cruelty are rampant.

I've spent the past four years trying to uncover the hidden culture of aggression in America's schools. Students, parents and school administrators have all pointed to Internet bullying as the latest, most vicious trend in children's social cruelty.

The Rise of Internet Bullying

About 45 million American kids ages 10 to 17 are currently estimated to be online, spending hours every day at their computers. With the click of a button, they can e-mail rumors to scores of recipients for instant viewing, permanently damaging a peer's reputation and social life. Instant messaging (IM) is equally treacherous. Like the calculating three-way phone call where one person remains silent, two girls can hover at the same computer screen, harvesting secrets from the messages of a hapless member of their "buddy" list. And when friendships sour, it is common for children to steal each others' passwords and break into e-mail, IM accounts and personal profiles, sending destructive messages under assumed identities.

Weblogs, or "blogs," are the latest sites of Internet cruelty. Blogs are cyber reality shows, widely read diaries that publicly detail the social drama and fluctuating emotions of young lives. They are often scoured for personal mention, and they spare no language or feelings.

One 12-year-old blogger, writing on the popular Angelfire Web site, recently announced she would devote her page to "anyone and everyone I hate and why." She minced no words. "erin used to be aka miss perfect. too bad now u r a train face. hahaha. god did that to u since u r such a b—. ashley stop acting like a slut wannabe. lauren u fat b— can't even go out at night w/ ur friends. . . . and laurinda u suck u god damn flat, weird voice, skinny as a stick b—."

Why Is Cyberbullying Increasing?

This isn't likely to be some child of poverty or deprivation speaking. Internet bullying involves a population that is largely middle-class, usually known as the "good kids" who are "on the right track" or, as many school personnel told me, "the ones you'd least expect" to bully or degrade others. The Internet foments outrageous behavior in part because it is a "gray area" for social interactions. Rebecca Kullback, a Montgomery County [Maryland] psychotherapist and former counselor at Sidwell Friends School in the District [of Columbia], believes the Internet deletes social inhibitions. "It allows kids to say and do things that they wouldn't do face-to-face, and they feel like they won't be held accountable in the same way. It gives them a false sense of security and power."

The kids themselves agree. "E-mails are so much less personal," says Elana Lowell, 18, a recent graduate of Charles E. Smith Jewish Day School in Rockville [Maryland]. "They're so much less formal and more indirect, and it's easier for people to be more candid and even meaner because of that. People can be as mean and vicious as they want because they're not directly confronting the person. It's the same thing as when you're talking on the phone because you don't have to face the person directly. This is a step further removed. You don't even have to hear the person's voice or see their reaction."

If things get heated online, adds Stephanie Herrold, a 16-year-old student at Churchill High School in Potomac [Maryland], teens "can just sign off and, when asked in person, act like nothing happened. They can even say that it was someone else on their screen name. They don't have to own their aggression."

Just as online cruelty may be intensified by the distance separating perpetrator and victim, it also changes the face of bullying itself. "Kids no longer have the safety of being able to go home and escape bullying," Kullback said. "Ten years ago, if a kid got bullied he could go home and sit in front of the TV." Nowadays, with children spending so much time on the computer, whether to shop, do research for schoolwork, play games or hang out with friends, Kullback says, they are easier to target for abuse. "Kids have access to one another 24 hours a day. They can bully each other at midnight."

Schools Are Not Responding

In all but the most disruptive situations, school officials disapprove but do little else, arguing that the acts occur off school grounds. Yet as every child knows, "juicy" material is quickly passed around, in print or by word-of-mouth, indelibly marking the fabric of the school community.

The proprietary nature of personal Web pages and blogs is pitting ethics against rights, or what kids know about bullying against what they know about personal freedom of speech and intellectual property.

Rosalind Wiseman, co-founder of the Washington [D.C.]-based Empower Program, a nonprofit organization that teaches anti-violence at schools nationwide, believes that administrators demur in part because they are intimidated by the technology being used. "So many principals do not understand the connection between e-mail that occurs at home and creating a safe environment in school," she says. "Adults' perceptions of kids are that they're so technology-savvy, and we, as people who aren't technology-savvy, have no ability to keep up. So we're just not going to try."

Where schools do intercede, new methods of investigation may be required. When two boys at Pyle Middle School in Bethesda [Maryland] devoted a Web site to pronouncing a classmate a "fag," school officials disciplined the boys and had them dismantle the site after a student notified the school. But not all cases are so clear-cut. As Robyn Jackson, a student support specialist at Pyle, told me, "Before there was the Internet, you could bring the bullies in. When the bullying goes online, you have to establish a paper trail. You have to get printouts. Oftentimes it's not archived." She added, "If a child is being bullied in the lunchroom or the hallway, typically children see it. Online, if there's no paper trail, no one sees it."

Most parents would not hesitate to assume responsibility for their child's behavior on a playground or at school, or in someone else's home. What happens online should be no different.

Cyberbullying Is Difficult to Control

In matters of discipline, the proprietary nature of personal Web page and blogs is pitting ethics against rights, or what kids know about bullying against what they know about personal freedoms of speech and intellectual property. When a child is reprimanded for negative or hateful speech on a personal Web page, she may invoke her right to write what she wants in a semi-private space. And the parents often go along. As Wiseman says, "Some parents are so concerned about respecting their children's rights that they see e-mail as a privacy issue." When a child is disciplined, the "parent has two reactions. One is, 'Who gave that to you?' And, 'These e-mails are the private property of my daughter. You can't admit that evidence into any court.'"

The best strategy for promoting ethical behavior online may be proactive. At Saint Ursula Academy, a Catholic girls' school in Cincinnati [Ohio], students sign an agreement at the beginning of the school year obligating them to ethical use of the Internet, e-mail and the school network. School policy puts teeth into the agreement by defining bullying as actionable whether it occurs on or off campus, in writing or in person. Online bullying may be punished with demerits that may lead to probation or dismissal.

As part of its School Violence Prevention Institute, Wiseman's Empower organization provides schools with help communicating anti-bullying policy to the school community. In a sample letter to parents and students, a school would prohibit "e-mails that include malicious gossip and slander, 'hit lists' via e-mail or other methods of communication naming specific students and/or teachers, [and] changing other people's e-mail [or] personal profiles." Consequences for these acts include suspension or removal from extracurricular activities or school itself.

School Officials and Parents Should Act

Education is just as critical. Most parents would not hesitate to assume responsibility for their child's behavior on a playground, at school, or in someone else's home. What happens online should be no different. Parents should talk with their children about computer ethics, stipulate rules of conduct, and—most importantly—establish computer consequences. They should instruct their children never to share their passwords or fight with someone online.

Classroom teachers can play an active role in instructing children about appropriate conduct online, even where there is no school policy on the issue. By promoting public discussion about their lives on the Internet, teachers and students can work together to share advice and develop "rules to type by" or similar Internet-minded guidance. Internet service providers such as AOL could develop software to monitor and regulate online socializing for children 13 and younger. Internet executives can help schools by establishing universal user guidelines for all children and their parents. Schools need to accept the reality of Internet cruelty and reevaluate, if not rewrite, their current policies on bullying.

The anti-pornography crusade successfully urged Internet providers to mount firewalls and other parental control devices to stop the young and sexually curious. Now, record executives are appealing to ethics to urge parents to stamp out pirating. Online social cruelty should be next.

Organizations to Contact

The editors have compiled the following list of organizations concerned with the issues debated in this book. The descriptions are derived from materials provided by the organizations. All have publications or information available for interested readers. The list was compiled on the date of publication of the present volume; the information provided here may change. Be aware that many organizations take several weeks or longer to respond to inquiries, so allow as much time as possible.

American Civil Liberties Union (ACLU)
125 Broad St., 18º Fl., New York, NY 10004
(888) 567-2258
Web site: www.aclu.org

The American Civil Liberties Union calls itself "our nation's guardian of liberty." It is usually held to be the foremost civil liberties organization in the United States. It has become involved in litigation and education on a wide variety of issues related to computer crime, including freedom of expression, Internet filtering, and privacy. Its Web site describes current news events, court cases, and legislation pertaining to its issues of interest. It will provide e-mail updates on the issues to members on request.

Berkman Center for Internet and Society
Harvard Law School, Cambridge, MA 02138
(617) 495-7547
e-mail: cyber@law.harvard.edu
Web site: cyber.law.harvard.edu

The Berkman Center was founded to study cyberspace and contribute to its development. Its primary activities include research and investigation of the boundaries in cyberspace between government, business, commerce, and education, and the relationship of the law to each of these areas. Its Web site includes a monthly newsletter, podcasts, and publications on its topics of interest, which include copyright, global innovation, digital learning, and online piracy.

Center for Democracy and Technology (CDT)
1634 I St. NW, Suite 1100, Washington, DC 20006
(202) 637-9800
Web site: www.cdt.org

The Center for Democracy and Technology promotes libertarian values such as free expression and privacy in issues involving the use of the Internet and other information technologies. Its Web site covers the Children's Online Protection Act and other legislation aimed at keeping young people away from content deemed unsuitable for them, spam, spyware, digital authentication, copyright and online piracy, cyberterrorism, and government surveillance. The site includes news items and descriptions of and comments on current legislation and court cases.

Coalition Against Unsolicited Commercial Email (CAUCE)
E-mail: comments@cauce.org
Web site: www.cauce.org

This volunteer organization was formed to address the worldwide problem of spam (unsolicited commercial e-mail). Through grassroots organizing, activism, and political lobbying, CAUCE supports legislative and other solutions that will result in the reduction or elimination of spam. Its Web site includes definitions and analysis of spam and its various effects on the Internet and Internet users, as well as press releases, policy papers, recent news reports, and other documents related to its topics of interest.

Computer Professionals for Social Responsibility (CPSR)
1370 Mission St., 4º Fl., San Francisco, CA 94103
(415) 839-9355
e-mail: cpsr@cpsr.org
Web site: www.cpsr.org

Founded in 1981, CPSR is a membership organization that works to educate government officials and computer users on issues including Internet governance, privacy and civil liberties, technology and ethics, and the global information society. Its Web site includes recent news, press releases, announcements, and other documents. An online action center provides information about upcoming events and activities, including an annual essay contest for students.

Electronic Frontier Foundation
454 Shotwell St., San Francisco, CA 94110
(415) 436-9333
e-mail: information@eff.org
Web site: www.eff.org

This organization, often described as "the ACLU of cyberspace," was founded in 1990 in response to an early federal hacker crackdown that threatened free speech by shutting down Web sites that were not involved in crimes. Since then the group has strongly advocated for privacy protection, public access to encryption technologies, and freedom of expression. It opposes Internet censorship or blocking, which is often proposed in the name of protecting children from pornography, and efforts by the recording industry and other copyright holders to overly restrict the fair use of their products. Its Web site covers court cases, legislation, and other news related to the organization's topics of interest and includes extensive links.

Electronic Privacy Information Center (EPIC)
1718 Connecticut Ave. NW, Suite 200
Washington, DC 20009
(202) 483-1140
Web site: www.epic.org

This group, established in 1994, focuses on the need to protect privacy and freedom of expression in the online world, both of which are closely related to cybercrime issues such as spam and e-mail fraud, identity theft, and Internet censorship aimed at protecting copyright holders or shielding children from pornography. The EPIC Web site includes reports and books, tracking of current legislation and court cases, and news stories. EPIC also offers a free newsletter, *EPIC Alert*, and links to related organizations. A separate Web site, www.privacy.org, presents additional news, information, and calls for action.

Federal Bureau of Investigation (FBI)
J. Edgar Hoover Building, Washington, DC 20535
(202) 324-3000
Web site: www.fbi.gov

The FBI is the chief criminal investigative agency of the U.S. government. Its Cyber Crimes Program handles computer-related offenses such as hacking and system attacks, theft of information, fraud, and online sexual predators. Its Crimes Against Children investigative program and the Innocent Images National Initiative focus on perpetrators of child pornography. Documents related to these programs can be accessed by typing the name of the program into the search engine on the FBI Web site.

Federal Trade Commission (FTC)
600 Pennsylvania Ave. NW, Washington, DC 20580
(202) 362-2222
Web site: www.ftc.gov

This government agency, founded in 1914, regulates business under federal law. One of its jobs is protecting consumers from misleading advertising, invasion of privacy, and fraud, including identity theft, whether these crimes involve computers or not. Material on identity theft, e-commerce and the Internet, and privacy can be found on the agency's Web site under the heading For Consumers: Consumer Information.

The Internet Society (ISOC)
International Secretariat, Reston, VA 20190
(703) 326-9880
Web site: www.isoc.org

The Internet Society is a nongovernmental organization with more than twenty thousand members in 180 countries. Its members include groups responsible for the maintenance of the Internet's infrastructure and standards, including the Internet Engineering Task Force and the Internet Architecture Board. The Internet Society maintains a clearinghouse for Internet information and education. Its Web site includes an Internet Code of Conduct section, with documents covering topics such as ethics and the Internet, site security, and guidelines for the conduct of Internet service providers.

National Fraud Information Center/Internet Fraud Watch
c/o National Consumers League, Washington, DC 20006
(202) 835-3323
e-mail: info@nclnet.org
Web site: www.fraud.org

The National Consumers League formed the National Fraud Information Center to educate consumers about telemarketing and Internet fraud. The center's Web site offers tips on common frauds and scams, including Internet fraud, scams against businesses, and counterfeit drugs (which are often sold over the Internet). The site includes an online form for reporting suspected fraud. A separate Web site focuses specifically on issues related to identity theft: www.phishinginfo.org.

Privacy International
London Headquarters, 6–8, Amwell St., London EC1R 1UQ
United Kingdom
(202) 470-0099 (U.S. phone)
e-mail: privacyint@privacy.org
Web site: www.privacyinternational.org

Privacy International is a nongovernmental organization with members in forty countries around the world. Its primary goal is to promote an international understanding of the importance of protecting individual privacy and personal data. Privacy International's Web site provides reports, studies, and commentary on current policy and technology issues, and also includes an online archive of information for students and researchers.

Save the Internet Coalition
c/o Free Press Action Fund, Northampton, MA 01061
(413) 585-1533
Web site: www.savetheinternet.com

Save the Internet is a coalition of individuals, organizations, and businesses that work to protect freedom of expression and fair access to the Internet for everyone. The coalition supports the Internet as a critical tool for economic growth, and opposes excessive governmental telecommunications legislation. Its Web site provides information on concepts such as network neutrality, which it calls "the Internet's First Amendment," recent news, and answers to basic questions about the effect of telecommunications law on the Internet.

U.S. Department of Justice, Criminal Division, Computer Crime and Intellectual Property Division
John C. Keeney Building, Washington, DC 20530
(202) 514-1026
Web site: www.cybercrime.gov

This section of the Department of Justice coordinates and provides resources for federal prosecution of computer crimes. Its Web site offers many resources, including descriptions of policy, cases, guidance, laws, and documents relating to computer crime, intellectual property crime, and computer ethics. Documents available on the site include press releases, speeches, testimony, reports, and manuals.

U.S. Secret Service
Office of Government Liaison and Public Affairs
Washington, DC 20223
(202) 406-5708
Web site: www.secretservice.gov

The U.S. Secret Service has historically been involved in the fight against counterfeiting. Today the agency helps to protect computers used in interstate commerce from cyberattacks. The Secret Service also investigates financial fraud, identity theft, and other crimes affecting the nation's financial, banking, and telecommunications infrastructure. The agency's Web site has a section containing the answers to questions frequently asked by students.

Bibliography

Books

Frances Cairncross	*The Death of Distance: How the Communications Revolution Is Changing Our Lives.* Boston: Harvard Business School Press, 2001.
CQ Researcher on Controversies in Law and Society	Washington, DC: CQ Press, 2001.
Sherri Mabry Gordon	*Downloading Copyrighted Stuff from the Internet: Stealing or Fair Use?* Berkeley Heights, NJ: Enslow Publishers, 2005.
Harry Henderson	*Internet Predators.* New York: Facts on File, 2005.
Doug Isenberg	*The GigaLaw Guide to Internet Law.* New York: Random House, 2002.
Kathryn Kolbert	*Justice Talking: Leading Advocates Debate Today's Most Controversial Issues—Censoring the Web.* New York: New Press, 2001.
Alan Marzilli	*Policing the Internet.* Philadelphia: Chelsea House, 2005.
Richard C. Monk	*Taking Sides: Clashing Views on Controversial Issues in Crime and Criminology*, 6th ed. Guilford, CT: Dushkin/McGraw-Hill, 2001.

Robert S. Peck — *Libraries, the First Amendment, and Cyberspace: What You Need to Know*. Chicago: American Library Association, 2000.

Aaron Schwabach — *Internet and the Law: Technology, Society, and Compromises*. Santa Barbara, CA: ABC-Clio, 2006.

David Wall — *Crime and the Internet*. New York: Routledge, 2001.

Art Wolinsky — *Safe Surfing on the Internet*. Berkeley Heights, NJ: Enslow, 2003.

Periodicals

Alex Adrianson — "Stopping Music Piracy Without Breaking the Internet: Digital Might Have a B-Side After All," *Consumers' Research Magazine*, October 2003.

Phillip Britt — "In the Wake of Security Breaches," *Information Today*, October 2005.

Richard C. Bulman Jr. and Jonathan Lehman — "Attacking the Hacking from the Inside Out," *Journal of Internet Law*, December 2004.

Jeff Chu — "You Wanna Take This Online? Cyberspace Is the 21st Century Bully's Playground Where Girls Play Rougher than Boys," *Time*, August 8, 2005.

Kurt Eichenwald — "From Their Own Online World, Pedophiles Extend Their Reach," *New York Times*, August 21, 2006.

Kurt Eichenwald — "Through His Webcam, a Boy Joins a Sordid Online World," *New York Times*, December 19, 2005.

Andrew Fano — "The New Internet Cops," *Computerworld*, September 8, 2003.

Dean Foust and Sonja Ryst — "ID Theft: More Hype than Harm; Law Enforcement Officials Say the Criminals Tend Not to Follow Through After Stealing Personal Data," *Business Week*, July 3, 2006.

Cara Garretson — "E-mail at a Crossroads: Spam, Phishing, and Other Abuses Are Threatening to Undermine Confidence in the Internet," *Network World*, November 1, 2004.

Joshua Green — "The Myth of Cyberterrorism," *Washington Monthly*, November 2002.

Amy Harmon — "As Digital Vandals Disrupt the Internet, aCall for Oversight," *New York Times*, September 1, 2003.

Jennifer Lee — "Identity Theft Victimizes Millions, Costs Billions," *New York Times*, September 4, 2003.

Steven Levy and Brad Stone — "Grand Theft Identity: Be Careful, We've Been Told, or You May Become a Fraud Victim. But Now It Seems that Corporations Are Failing to Protect Our Secrets. How Bad Is the Problem, and How Can We Fix It?" *Newsweek International*, September 5, 2005.

Adam Liptak	"Are There Civil Rights in Cyberspace? Internet Sites Can Legally Post Discriminatory, False, or Libelous Information from Users. Is It Time to Better Police the Web?" *New York Times Upfront*, April 24, 2006.
Bob Meadows	"The Web: The Bully's New Playground: With a New Arsenal of Web Sites and Chat Rooms, Mean Kids Can Torment Their Victims 24/7 Online—Often with Devastating Results," *People*, March 14, 2005.
Scott Medintz	"Talkin' 'Bout MySpace Generation: Kids' Online Profiles Can Hurt Job Prospects Decades Down the Road," *Money*, February 1, 2006.
Cade Metz	"The Sorry State of Security: Time to Face Facts: When It Comes to Our Online Safety Woes, Everybody Is to Blame," *PC Magazine*, February 21, 2006.
Pamela Paul	"The Porn Factor: In the Internet Age, Pornography Is Almost Everywhere You Look. But What Is It Doing to Real-Life Relationships?" *Time*, January 19, 2004.
Amanda Paulson	"Schools Grapple with Policing Students' Online Journals," *Christian Science Monitor*, February 2, 2006.
Lisa Pemberton	"Staying Safe While Networking on Web," *Olympian*, November 27, 2005.

Matthew Quirk	"The Web Police: Internet Censorship Is Prevalent Not Just in China but Throughout the World. Can the Web Be Tamed?" *Atlantic Monthly*, May 2006.
Robin Raskin	"The First Amendment vs. Internet Safety," *Family PC*, February 2000.
Julie Rawe	"How Safe Is MySpace?" *Time*, July 3, 2006.
Andrew Romano	"Walking a New Beat: Surfing MySpace.com Helps Cops Crack the Case," *Newsweek*, April 24, 2006.
Michael Rothschild	"The Threat from Within: The Evolution of Cyber Attacks," *Computer Technology Review*, March–April 2006.
Ira Sager, Ben Elgin, Peter Elstrom, Faith Keenan, and Pallavi Gogoi	"The Underground Web: Drugs, Gambling, Terrorism, Child Pornography. How the Internet Makes Any Illegal Activity More Accessible than Ever," *Business Week*, September 2, 2002.
Bruce Sterling	"CSI: The Net: One Observer's Take on Why the Internet Is the Biggest Crime Scene in History—Plus Expert Advice on Cleaning It Up (The New Security War: Internet Crime)," *Australian PC World*, February 12, 2006.
Jon Swartz	"Schoolyard Bullies Get Nastier Online," *USA Today*, March 7, 2005.

David Talbot	"Terror's Server," *Technology Review*, February 2005.
Dan Tynan	"The Internet Is Sick . . . But We Can Make It Better," *Popular Science*, October 2006.

Internet Sources

Brian Alexander	"The Thrill of Putting It All Out There: For Exhibitionists, the Internet Is an Ideal Fantasy Playground," December 1, 2006. (www.msnbc.msn.com/id/14061673)
American Civil Liberties Union	"The Seven Reasons Why the Senate Should Reject the International Cybercrime Treaty," December 18, 2003. (www.aclu.org/privacy/internet/14861res20031218.html)
Anne Broache	"Anticrime Group Calls for Laws to Curb 'Cyberbullying,'" August 17, 2006. (http://news.com.com/Anticrime+group+calls+for+laws+to+curb+cyberbullying/2100-1028_3-6106920.html)
Alan Docherty	"Anatomy of an Internet Porn Panic," October 15, 2004. (www.netfreedom.org/news.asp?item=213)
Jacqueline Emigh	"Online Transactions, Online Risks," *Government Security*, August 1, 2005. (http://govtsecurity.com/mag/online_transactions_online)

Jacqueline Emigh	"Terror on the Internet," *Government Security*, October 1, 2004. (http://govtsecurity.com/mag/terror_internet/index.html)
Alison George	"Living Online: The End of Privacy?" September 18, 2006. (www.newscientisttech.com/channel/tech/mg19125691.700-living-online-the-end-of-privacy.html)
Jack M. Germain	"Identity Theft Online: Debunking the Myths," January 17, 2004. (www.technewsworld.com/story/32622.html)
Jack M. Germain	"Will Antiphishing Legislation Be Effective?" November 13, 2004. (www.ecommercetimes.com/story/38006.html)
Jack M. Germain	"Scientist Blames Web Security Issues on Repeated Mistakes," May 24, 2005. (www.ecommercetimes.com/story/43233.html)
Jack M. Germain	"Online Privacy Regulations Forcing Better Handling of Data," July 16, 2005. (www.technewsworld.com/story/44560.html)
Charlene G. Gianetti and Margaret Sagarese	"The Newest Breed of Bully: The Cyberbully," undated. (www.pta.org/pr_magazine_article_details_1117639656218.html)

Grant Gross — "Does the Internet Need Its Own Police?" *PC World*, June 8, 2004. (www.pcworld.com/article/id,116440/article.html)

Alex Halperin — "No Space for MySpace? A Proposed Law Banning Social Networks from Computers in Schools and Libraries Could Block Access to a Huge Slice of the Net—Without Protecting Kids," May 12, 2006. (www.businessweek.com/technology/content/may2006/tc20060512_299340.htm)

Jessi Hempel — "From MySpace to Safer Space?" April 11, 2006. (www.businessweek.com/technology/content/apr2006/tc20060411_341338.htm)

Chris Peregrine — "Scrubbing the Internet Clean," March 2, 2005. (www.netfreedom.org/news.asp?item=216)

Paul Rothman — "How Can We Protect Our Critical Infrastructure from Cyber-Attack?" *Government Security*, May 1, 2003. http://govtsecurity.com/mag/protect_critical_infrastructure/index.html)

Rob Stafford — "Why Parents Must Mind MySpace," April 5, 2006. (www.msnbc.msn.com/id/11064451)

Loren Steffy	"The Most Dangerous Predator of All Lurks Online," April 14, 2006. (www.chron.com/disp/story.mpl/business/steffy/3793073.html)
Bob Sullivan	"Kids, Blogs, and Too Much Information," April 29, 2005. (www.msnbc.msn.com/id/7668788)
Michael Thompson	"My Turn Online: Leave Kids Alone on the Web," September 14, 2006. (www.msnbc.msn.com/id/14840599/site/newsweek)

Index

J

K

L

M

T

U

V

W

Y

Z